UNDERSTANDING
THE FEASTS OF THE LORD

By Dr. Roger V. Houtsma

Published by

World Outreach
P.O. Box 950
Novato, CA 94948

Cover designed by Tenney Singer

i

UNDERSTANDING
THE FEASTS OF THE LORD

ISBN 0-9617623-0-6

Printed in the United States of America

TABLE OF CONTENTS

FORWARD

I believe that we are entering the greatest hour for the church in history! God is releasing His Spirit in a wonderful outpouring throughout our world to bring His purposes and intentions for the church to completion. As the church continues to grow in relationship with God and through new consecrations and faith appropriations of the resurrected Life of Jesus Christ, the world will be touched by the greatest manifestation of the power and glory of God that it has ever seen.

The emphasis in this last-day outpouring is upon one's relation- ship with God. All true meaning in life is found in relationships, and all true ministry is born out of one's personal relationship with Christ. The study of the Feasts of the Lord reveals a progressive unfolding pattern of truth and development for the believer seeking to go on to completion of God's purposes in his life and the church. With the understanding gained through the Word, the believer is more able to cooperate with the working of the Holy Spirit to become all that the Lord has intended him to be.

Too often our emphasis has been upon knowledge and learning some new thing, whereas the Lord's emphasis has been upon our relationship with Him so that we may become one with Christ as He is with the Father — manifesting His wisdom, His nature, His power and His glory. May the Lord use this study to open your heart to greater dimensions of relationship with our Lord who loves us more than we can ever imagine!

Roger Houtsma

THE SEVEN FEASTS OF THE LORD

NAME	DATE	PAST/MEMORIAL
I . 1) PASSOVER	14th of Abib at evening	Israel freed from Egypt's bondage
2) Unleavened Bread	15th-22nd of Abib	Fleeing Egypt in haste
3) Firstfruits	Sunday of the week	Go to meet with God, firstfruit given to God
II . 4) PENTECOST (Harvest, Weeks)	Sunday after 7th sabbath, or 50 days after Firstfruits	Mt. Sinai - God speaks in an audible voice to nation of Israel - Giving of 10 commandments
III . TABERNACLES 5) Trumpets	1st day of 7th month	Entering into promised land of Canaan
6) Day of Atonement	10th day of 7th month	High priest offers for sins of all Israel in Holy of Holies
7) Booths (Tabernacles, Harvest)	15th-22nd day of 7th month	Commemorates Israel in wilderness

PROPHETIC	PERSONAL	SEASONAL (Waves of Restoration)
Christ's death on Calvary	Salvation, justification Romans 1-5	Martin Luther saved by grace through faith
Christ's burial	Righteousness imputed, sanctification Romans 6 & 7 Buried with Him	Conrad Grebel, Felix Manz Anabaptists
Christ's resurrection	Holiness Romans 6:11 Romans 8 Raised with Him	Moody, Wesley, Finney - holiness movement
Outpouring of Holy Spirit - Acts 2	Baptism in Holy Spirit	1906 Azusa Wales Pentecostal outpouring
Israel becomes a nation, gathering of church	Call to holiness, personal sanctification Fourfold: 1) Call out of tribes 2) Move to keep feasts 3) Call to war 4) Celebrate feasts	Charismatic Renewal 1967 Jerusalem captured 1973 Yom Kipppur War 1980 Jerusalem annexed - Call to Day of Atonement
Soul affliction, tribulation	Righteousness implemented, preparing for glory of God, sin out of camp	Is upon us
Full manifestation of Kingdom in all the earth, all Israel saved	This feast is soon coming to fulfillment in seven parts: (1) unity; (2) joy; (3) rest; (4) ingathering; (5) glory; (6) restoration; (7) His appearing in us, then for us	

THE FEASTS OF THE LORD

There were three feast periods in the year for the Jew under the covenant of the law. The first period (the Feast of Unleavened Bread) had three feasts held over a period of one week. These feasts were called Passover, Feast of Unleavened Bread and Firstfruits. These are all described more specifically in Leviticus Chapter 23. This first feast period took place during the first month on the Jewish lunar calendar, which is around the time that we celebrate Easter.

The second feast period, Pentecost (Feast of Weeks), was 50 days from Passover and took place in the third month.

The third feast period (the Feast of Tabernacles) began with the Feast of Trumpets in the seventh month. Ten days later came the most holy day on the Jewish calendar, which was the Day of Atonement, immediately followed by the Feast of Booths, or Tabernacles.

The first four feasts really govern the first advent of the Lord Jesus Christ. This includes the incarnation of our Lord, His death, burial, resurrection and the outpouring of the Holy Spirit. The last three feasts govern the events of the second advent of Christ, which we will see from several aspects.

> Three times in a year shall all thy males appear before the Lord thy God in the place which he shall choose; in the feast of unleavened bread, and in the feast of weeks, and in the feast of tabernacles: and they shall not appear before the Lord empty: Every man shall give as he is able, according to the blessing of the Lord thy God which he hath given thee. Deut. 16:16–17

It was part of the law that the Israelites, in keeping the feasts, had to come giving. The men were specifically mentioned because, as the heads of the household, it was very important that the spiritual leaders participated in and were aware of what these events were all about.

> Three times thou shalt keep a feast unto me in the year. Thou shalt keep the feast of unleavened bread (thou shalt eat unleavened bread seven days, as I commanded thee, in the time appointed of the month of Abib; for in it thou camest out from Egypt: and none shall appear before me empty). And the feast of harvest, the firstfruits of thy labours, which thou hast sown in the field: and the feast of ingathering, which is

in the end of the year, when thou hast gathered in thy labours out of the field. Three times in the year all thy males shall appear before the Lord God. Thou shalt not offer the blood of my sacrifice with unleavened bread; neither shall the fat of my sacrifice remain until the morning. The first of the firstfruits of thy land thou shalt bring into the house of the Lord thy God. Thou shalt not seethe a kid in his mother's milk.
Ex. 23:14–19

Thrice in the year shall all your menchildren appear before the Lord God, the God of Israel. For I will cast out the nations before thee, and enlarge thy borders: neither shall any man desire thy land, when thou shalt go up to appear before the Lord thy God thrice in the year. Ex. 34:23–24

God promised to protect the land as the men left their homes to go to Jerusalem in order to keep the feasts. He also promised to drive out their enemies, which is a promise of deliverance.

Each of these feasts was considered to be a holy convocation unto the Lord under the law and has a special significance and meaning for us in four different ways: a past memorial aspect in the history of Israel; a prophetic aspect involving Christ and Israel; a personal application in our lives; and a seasonal application, which is also prophetic in nature, for the church.

The Past Memorial Aspect

Passover was when Israel was brought out of Egypt. You remember the night of the Passover when Moses had the final declaration from God through which Israel would be released from Egypt. The death angel would pass through the land and the first-born of all of the animals and the people in Egypt would die, but those who were inside the houses of the Hebrew children with the blood applied over the door post would be protected from death. They were to eat the lamb and unleavened bread, their loins girded ready to go. They would then march out on the next day to keep an appointment with the Lord at Mount Sinai. This is now a past, historical event.

Fifty days later Israel arrived at Mount Sinai and the first Pentecost. God visibly descended upon that mountain in a flame of fire and smoke and spoke audibly to the entire nation. Here the glory of the Lord was revealed, along with the pattern for the tabernacle of Moses and worship of the Lord.

Trumpets, Day of Atonement and Booths came with this pattern of worship and began to be kept in the wilderness. These feasts were kept year after year as required of God under the law. When the feasts were kept, the father of the household was to sit down and explain to the entire household how God brought the children of Israel out of Egypt, all of the supernatural interventions that took place and what these rituals teach of God.

The prophetic aspect

These feasts were also prophetic, and this is one of the reasons why God required that they keep them every year. Not only did God want them to remember what He had done in the beginning but all the things that were done then pointed forward to something much greater that would come to pass in Israel's future. It would be a means by which their understanding could be opened to receive, understand and accept that greater thing which God had promised, THE COMING OF THE MESSIAH. The prophetic fulfillment came when Christ, our Passover Lamb who met every aspect of the law and requirement for a lamb sacrificed for sin, was crucified on the day of Passover; on the day of Unleavened Bread He was buried in the grave; on the day that the beginning of the Feast of Firstfruits took place, He rose from the grave in the mighty resurrection; and 50 days later, when all the people of Israel had come to Jerusalem to keep the Feast of Pentecost, the Baptism of the Holy Spirit was poured out in the upper room. This was the first advent governed by the first four feasts. The prophetic fulfillment of the last three feasts governing the second advent is beginning to come to pass for the first time today.

It's not by accident that these things were fulfilled. There are at least 334 Messianic prophecies fulfilled in the first advent of Christ, the probability of which is inconceivable. Ten of them being fulfilled in proper order would have the probability of one in ten billion. Make it 11 and it would be one in one hundred billion. It wasn't by chance that these events were brought to pass.

Trumpets' prophetic fulfillment was the regathering of Israel as a nation, which has been taking place in our generation. You and I are witnesses of that in this hour.

The Day of Atonement is a day of soul affliction and great tribulation for Israel. In the events of Israel prophetically, it deals with the tribulation period, which will soon be upon us. It has a different aspect of application to the Body of Christ. The seed of Abraham is both spiritual and physical. The natural seed is the children of Israel. But as Jesus spoke to the Pharisees who said they could trace their genealogy all the way back to Abraham, He said, "If you were the children of Abraham you would do the works of Abraham, but you do the works of your father who is the devil. He is the father of all lies."

The Tabernacles fulfillment is to come as the full manifestation of the Kingdom on the earth, which is the millennial period.

The personal aspect

We have a personal application to receive from each of these feasts. First, we can only enter into the Kingdom of God when we keep the Passover and the blood of Christ is applied in our life, and we are justified by faith; we must be born again with the blood applied. Until then, we are outside the Kingdom of God. Second, the Feast of Unleavened Bread and Firstfruits represents water baptism, an expression by which the old man is buried to set us free from the old life. We are then raised up to walk in newness of life. We then need to go on and keep the Feast of Pentecost personally, where we receive the Baptism of the Holy Spirit. Once one of these feasts has been kept for the church and has been kept in fulfillment with Christ for the believer, then it is available throughout the church age. The remaining three feasts are apparently to be fulfilled in our day. The truths that they hold for us will be manifest seasonally as the church keeps these events.

The seasonal aspect

The first four feasts have been fulfilled in their seasonal aspect as the church was born. The last three feasts are now coming into this seasonal view. Trumpets deals with coming out of our tribes (denominations) to meet with the whole body. The charismatic renewal that took place in the mid-60's and 70's was an expression of the keeping of the Feast of Trumpets, and its parallel with the events of Israel is astonishing. The prophetic timetable in God's Word as it is revealed in world events and the Body of Christ today makes it easy to see that we are on our way right now to keeping the Day of Atonement, followed by Tabernacles. These things have never been kept and are just now coming to pass.

This is a day when our ears need to be opened to hear and receive truth. The Day of Atonement is a revelation that is being translated into experience. For Jesus' doctrine to be translated into experiential reality for His disciples, He had to die on Calvary. There are some things that have to take place in the life of the believer in order for righteousness, which was imputed at Passover, to be implemented at the Day of Atonement. Please notice when you see this progressive development in a walk with God that the Day of Atonement is not a repeat of Passover. There is something much greater to take place here.

Tabernacles represents entering into the full redemptive experience of Calvary — full victory over sin, full expression of Christ in us, culminating in the rapture of the church and the coming of the Lord.

> These are the feasts of the Lord, even holy convocations, which ye shall proclaim in their seasons. Lev. 23:4

> And I will pour upon the house of David and upon the inhabitants of Jerusalem the spirit of grace and supplication. And they shall look upon me whom they have pierced and they shall mourn for him as one mourns for his only son and shall be in bitterness for him as one that is in bitterness for his first born. Zech. 12:10

This is a prophecy for Israel when they begin to recognize that Christ was genuinely their Messiah.

> But one of the soldiers with a spear pierced his side and forthwith came out blood and water. And he that saw it bore record and his record is true and he knows that what he saith is true that you might believe. For these things were done, that the scripture should be fulfilled, A bone of him shall not be broken. And again another scripture saith, They shall look on him whom they pierced. John 19:34–37

> Behold, he cometh with clouds; and every eye shall see him, and they also which pierced him: and all kindreds of the earth shall wail because of him. Even so, Amen. Rev. 1:7

Please understand that although Jesus came in the incarnation as the Lamb of God, He is not returning as the Lamb of God. In the second coming of Christ, He will come as the Mighty Lion of the Tribe of Judah and vengeance will be in His hand. He will smite them by the Word of His mouth, the Word of the Lord, a sword that divides asunder between soul and spirit and joints and marrow, and justice shall be meted out. Those who have rejected the Christ, and the antichrist (who will have come up into his kingdom and ruled the world) will be judged by God and righteousness will reign on the earth. You cannot have righteousness without judging unrighteousness. You cannot have forgiveness without judging sin; you must be judged guilty to have forgiveness.

Christ is coming and it is not going to be as everyone expects. People say, "Well, God is never going to judge sin." God, in His mercy, withholds judgment to give man a space of time to repent, to be forgiven and to be rightly related to Him, but those who refuse will be judged.

We must recognize that people do not go to hell because they sin. Most people do not understand what causes a person to go to eternal damnation, but Jesus made it very clear:

> And this is the condemnation, that light is come into the world, and men loved darkness rather than light, because their deeds were evil. And they would not come to the light, lest they be reproved. But he that comes to the light, he does so that his deeds might be made manifest, that they are wrought in God.
> John 3:19-21

What is the condemnation? What brings a person to eternal damnation? Not the fact that he is a sinner, but the fact that he refuses to be delivered from that sin. He refuses to accept God's deliverance and forgiveness, and that refusal leaves God no choice. When we talk about judgment in this day and age, we've had so much humanistic teaching in our public school system, in our media and in the entertainment industries that it's a shock to think that God would ever judge. We were made in the image of God, and every loving parent judges his child every time he disciplines him for his well being.

As we are looking at this seasonal aspect, we must recognize that God is following the pattern of the feasts in His restoration of the church. The church was born in power and glory. As she kept these first four feasts, the power of God was manifested and that generation saw many wonderful things. Then something happened. There was a progression where the church began to die out from spiritual reality. There was a major change as the teaching of the Judaizers and Gnostics mixed into the teaching of the church. When Constantine became Emperor, he declared that the religion of Rome was Christianity, a marriage of church and state. The result was that all kinds of heathen priests claimed they were Christian and continued their own rites, and many of the people who did not know Christ claimed to be Christian. People who didn't even know God began to arise as leaders in the church. Deterioration continued until in the Dark Ages you see things like the Spanish Inquisition where genuine Christians were martyred by the church.

The day came when a change began to take place, and out of it came a man raised up by God named Martin Luther. His message was one of Passover. He began to search the Scripture until he found the Word of the Lord in the Old Testament that said the just shall live by faith. He realized that salvation doesn't come by kissing a piece of wood or going through the ritualism of the church, so he put up his great edict. The major message of Martin Luther was back to Passover and faith in our Passover Lamb for salvation, and the Reformation began.

Soon following was another wave of restoration and truth in the church, the message of the Feast of Unleavened Bread. The Wesleys then brought the church into the sanctification message. Along with them were the Anabaptists and their concepts of water baptism, followed by a new wave taken as the Firstfruits message with the positive aspect of holiness – walking in newness of life. People like D. L. Moody and Charles Finney preached the message of "let's change the way we live!" That message went all across the country in the 1800's.

In the early part of this century another wave took place, the Pentecostal outpouring in Wales and on Azusa Street, in Kansas City, in Seattle, in India, in Africa, in Sweden, in Europe and in South America. Within a three-year period of time, God sovereignly poured out His Spirit all over this world and the message of the Baptism in the Holy Spirit with speaking in other tongues was struck on fire. The Pentecostal

Revival took place and the Feast of Pentecost was kept. That message has been growing and has caused the greatest missionary work and harvest to take place which has been seen since the early church.

A group of Catholics had a retreat, where they were going to study the person and work of the Holy Spirit. (Up until that time, many who became Pentecostals were rejected by their part of the Body of Christ. Many Pentecostal gatherings were stoned, had tomatoes thrown at them, etc. It was typical of every wave. Luther was rejected by the existing body. Those who kept Unleavened Bread were rejected by the existing body, as were those who kept Firstfruits and Pentecost.) At the retreat house they tried to turn on the water, but it wouldn't flow. They decided to join hands and pray that God would turn the water on. They prayed and believed that God would answer the prayer and said, "Thank you, Lord, for answering the prayer and fixing the water." After they finished thanking the Lord, they turned on the tap and the water flowed. God answered their prayer, but not just to make the water flow. The principle illustrated here is what they discovered in the Scripture when they began to study the person and work of the Holy Spirit and the message of the Baptism of the Holy Spirit. When they had seen this event in answer to prayer and saw these principles taught in the Word concerning the Baptism of the Holy Spirit, they applied them and sovereignly received the Baptism, and the Charismatic Renewal was born.

The Charismatic Renewal was the Feast of Trumpets, but it was without leaders. It was the only wave so far that didn't have a group of a few men who could be looked to as the leadership of the movement. It was sovereign and reached into every denomination of the Body of Christ. When you understand the meaning of Trumpets, you see that one of the things Trumpets was to do was to call the children of Israel out of their 12 tribes to meet at the tent of assembly where God would speak to them. That means we are to come out of being Catholic, Methodist, Pentecostal, Baptist, etc. If someone tells me, "I'm a Bapticostal, a Catholic Charismatic, a Lutheran Charismatic," I say, "Well, I'm a Charismatic Hindu!" It makes just about as much sense to me. I don't care what your background is, you need to drop your nametag and be a Christian and identify with the Body of Christ.

This feast has been and is being kept today for the first time in history, which means that right in its wake are Atonement and Tabernacles. When you begin to study the Word of God prophetically and to interpret it in relationship to events that are unfolding like this, you begin to see things in the natural and the spiritual as a parallel. **All of these events had their parallel in natural Israel.** They are also very literal — they have a past historical, memorial aspect; they are prophetic because they had a greater literal fulfillment to come; they're personal because they are spiritually applied to us; and they are seasonal, dealing with the time periods through which God is moving in the earth.

How do we know that these seasons are right? How do we know this is the hour that God speaks of in His Word as the generation that will see the second coming of Christ? There are many different ways we can know that, but I want to share with you some of those parallels with the events in Israel in this century. What is happening in Israel in the natural is an exact parallel with what is happening in the Body of Christ. "Howbeit that was not first which is spiritual, but that which is natural; and afterward that which is spiritual" (I Cor. 15:46).

Zionism began to build around the time the Lord was restoring to the church the truths of Firstfruits and Pentecost. The first advent is governed by these feasts. World War I was from 1914 to 1917, which was the first earth-shaking catastrophe that was ever called a world war. That was a sign of the times because Jesus said you will see wars and rumors of wars, and nation will rise against nation, and there will be perplexity and men's hearts will fail them for fear in these last days. Perplexity literally means "no way out."

It was during this time that we observe a change of leadership and direction in the world, as well as a change of leadership and direction in the Body of Christ. General Allenby of the British Army marched into Jerusalem, which had been occupied by the Turkish Army for approximately 400 years, and took the entire city without one shot. Why? The Turkish general saw a sign in the heavens and interpreted that it was God's will to evacuate the city. The British Empire proceeded to proclaim Palestine a national homeland for the Jews who had been wandering ever since 70 A.D., when Titus destroyed Jerusalem. They were free to

9

return from anywhere in the world, and it was God's door of escape for the things that would come upon the Jews in Nazi Germany. However, they didn't return to Palestine because they felt too comfortable where they were.

The parallel in the church was the birth of the Pentecostal denominations — the Four Square Church, the Assemblies of God, etc. The Pentecostal Movement began to grow and has become the third major force in Christendom.

Following World War II, in 1946–47 the Jews wanted to leave Europe after the overthrow of Hitler. Ezekiel had prophesied it. He looked into the Valley of Dry Bones and saw they were parched and baked. It was a picture that the prophet Ezekiel saw hundreds of years before of what would happen in Nazi Germany, where graves had been dug open and those cooked bones from the ovens were pushed in by the thousands and covered over with dirt. He looked down the telescope of time upon the nation of Israel, which was almost extinct, and the Word of the Lord came to him and said:

And he said unto me, Son of man, can these bones live? And I answered, O Lord God, thou knowest. Again he said unto me, Prophesy upon these bones, and say unto them, O ye dry bones, hear the word of the Lord. Thus saith the Lord God unto these bones; Behold, I will cause breath to enter into you, and ye shall live. So I prophesied as I was commanded: and as I prophesied, there was a noise, and behold a shaking, and the bones came together, bone to his bone. And when I beheld, lo, the sinews and flesh came up upon them, and the skin covered them above: but there was no breath in them. Then said he unto me, Prophesy unto the wind, prophesy, son of man, and say to the wind, thus saith the Lord God; come from the four winds, O breath, and breathe upon these slain, that they may live. So I prophesied as he commanded me, and the breath came into them, and they lived, and stood up upon their feet an exceeding great army. Then he said unto me, Son of man, these bones are the whole house of Israel: behold, they say, Our bones are dried, and our hope is lost: we are cut off for our parts. Therefore prophesy and say unto them, Thus saith the Lord God; Behold, O my people, I will open your graves, and cause you to come up out of your graves, and bring you into the land of Israel. And ye shall know that I am the Lord, when I have opened your graves, O my people, and brought you up out of your graves, and shall put my spirit in you, and ye shall live, and I shall place you in your own land: then shall ye know that I the Lord have spoken it, and performed it, saith the Lord. Ezek. 37:2–5,7–14

This was a prophecy of the restoration and revitalization of Israel. That prophecy began to find its fulfillment right after World War II. When the Jews began to arrive in Israel, they faced Arab troops who were there to keep them out. God raised a man named Ben–Gurion who stood up and shook his finger at the United Nations Council and proclaimed that Israel would be their land again. The English played both sides against the middle, but the Jews won and for the first time in over 2500 years Israel was formed as a sovereign country when, in 1948, the United Nations made a resolution to recognize her as a nation. They don't know to this day why they made that resolution. The Palestinians have been squirming over it ever since, but God was in it.

Along with that major prophetic event coming to pass, there was a parallel in the church. **Great evangelists reached national prominence overnight.** There was a small meeting of about 300 people a few weeks later in a tent. A man named Billy Graham was preaching in Los Angeles. The owner of the Hearst newspapers showed up, decided he liked Billy Graham and told all of his papers across the country, "Puff Graham," and he was catapulted from a mediocre–sized evangelist into national prominence overnight. A man named William Branham arose in a major miracle ministry. T. L. Osborn was born out of Branham's ministry, as was Oral Roberts. At one time in the early 1950's, there were over 200 healing evangelists traveling across this nation, and the miracle power of God was manifest all over this country. This was another wave of the Pentecostal Revival. Unfortunately, many of these individuals became casualties because they didn't have character foundations in their lives as the gifts of the Spirit were restored to the church.

At the same time the **Latter Rain Movement** began to be born. It came into disrespect very early because of problems with the leadership; nevertheless, it unleashed a new dimension of God's power. **There was also a change in leadership.** In the 1940's major leaders were gathered home: Dr. Charles Price, Amy Semple McPherson, Smith Wigglesworth, and a new dimension of leadership was brought into the Body of Christ.

I want you to see a pattern here. There was a major event in World War I from 1914 to 1917; there were approximately 30 years between 1915 and 1946, and 20 years from 1946 to 1966. In June, 1967 the Six Day War took place with hardly a shot fired. The Arabs rose up, the Israelis marched out and the Arabs, who had huge tanks, suddenly turned around and left. A handful of Israeli soldiers went into cities where the radios were still on and cooking was on the stove, but there wasn't a person in town. When asked why they left, the people said, "We saw this great massive army around us," but there had been only 50 men. What did they see? Why did they go? God gave the Israelis the city, the Golan Heights and the West Bank. Old Jerusalem, for the first time in over 2000 years, became a part of the nation of Israel. In August of 1980, Jerusalem would become the official capital of Israel. These events fulfill Jesus' prophecy, "And they shall fall by the edge of the sword, and shall be led away captive into all nations: and Jerusalem shall be trodden down of the Gentiles, until the times of the Gentiles be fulfilled" (Luke 21:24).

What happened in the church during that time? An Orthodox priest was airlifted to the top of Mount Sinai, where he blew a ram's horn which, according to Isaiah, signified that the Feast of Trumpets was going to be kept. The parallel we have seen in the church was the beginning of the Charismatic Renewal. New leadership went into motion. People like Kathryn Kuhlman were catapulted into national prominence during that time. The Charismatic Renewal began to flow throughout this country and around the world. Even the Pope put his blessings on the Catholic Charismatic movement, unheard of in the past.

The Yom Kippur War took place in 1973, which was drawing our attention to the Day of Atonement. It was an announcement to underscore Trumpets being fulfilled with its call to go on to keep the Day of Atonement. The Yom Kippur War was a dress rehearsal of Gog and Magog in Ezekiel 37, 38 and 39. Before Jesus comes, Russia, through the Arab surrogates with which it works, will come against Israel and God will sovereignly intervene.

When we came to Marin County in 1976, we had already been prophesying for two years that there would be a major change in the Middle East at the time of the Feast of Tabernacles in November of 1978. It would not be by war and there would be a new alignment of nations. This was brought to pass in 1978 when Anwar Sadat of Egypt proposed his peace initiative and a realignment of nations resulted.

It was during the time of the peace initiative that Kathryn Kuhlman was brought home. The Charismatic Renewal has waned; it's not what God is doing today. God is now taking us from Trumpets to the Day of Atonement, or righteousness implemented. People who are back there just keeping Passover don't have the manifest presence and glory of God with them. They are saved, but have stopped short of what God is doing in this hour. God is taking us somewhere. Notice the pattern: 30 years, 20 years, and 10 years in 1978. For four years God showed us that in the Spring of 1982 there would be a spiritually significant war in Israel around the time of Passover, followed by a new wave of God's restoring work in the church. The Israeli–Lebanese War took place at that time and a new dimension of God's moving in the Body of Christ is emerging.

These events are all part of the seasonal aspect of the message of the Feasts as we study them in the Scripture. Remember, they have a past, historical, memorial aspect; they have a literal prophetic aspect for Israel; they have a personal, spiritual aspect applied to us; and they have a seasonal aspect of what God is doing in the earth — all easily identified in the world from the Scripture. A study of the Feasts is vital because for the first time in the history of the world, the events that were prophesied and pictured by this feast period of Tabernacles, governing the second coming of Christ, are coming to pass. We are living as the most privileged people who ever walked the face of the earth. People say, "Oh, I would love to have lived when Jesus walked the earth in the flesh, watched Him feed the multitude and talked to Him." Let me tell you, the people who lived then would have given anything to trade places with you and live in the day when these things will come to pass.

There isn't a word in the Scripture that isn't true. There isn't a prophecy in the Scripture that isn't coming to pass perfectly in order. Sixty-six books, many different authors from different generations and different cultures and countries, different languages — everything they say perfectly harmonizes and amplifies the revelation of God in the earth. If you want to question this, all you have to do is look at the world events around you and there is one thing you will have to admit, it's in the Book.

There are two things by which Jesus gave credibility to His identity: (1) prophecy which was fulfilled from the Scripture; (2) the miracles, signs and wonders which He did. One alone is not enough, both are needed for out of the mouth of two or three witnesses is every word established. This is why a study of the Feasts is so important. God wants to take us on to completion.

When I first got saved, I was appalled at how little most people knew about the Word of God. I had no Christian background; I didn't even know the story of David and Goliath, so every time I went to church it was brand new. I began to study the Word six to eight hours a day and soaked it up. I found out after I had been a Christian for a short time that I knew more than many people who had been Christians for several years because they hadn't taken the time to study the Book and follow through with what God was saying. I had this attitude: "If you don't want to be spiritual, you can stay where you are, but I'm going all the way with God. I'll go off and be spiritual all by myself." God spoke to me one day and began to let me see that I could never find fulfillment of what He intended for my life without the Body of Christ, nor could any believer. I said, "Lord, I understand why you spoke this way to Israel — stiffnecked, stubborn, murmuring and rebellious." It was funny to find out I was like that, too!

This drew my attention to two men who I really respect, Joshua and Caleb. They went forth and spied out the land. God showed them what was there for them, they tasted of the fruit of the land and it was wonderful. There were a few giants out there, but Caleb said, "That's OK, they're just meant to be bread for us, they'll make us grow strong in the Spirit." All the Johnny Milktoasts stood up and said, "Wait a minute now, those giants will make us like grasshoppers, they'll destroy us, so let's hide in the wilderness." Israel followed and because of that, they wandered another 38 years in the wilderness. Joshua and Caleb believed God to go in and they were ready, but God said to them, "You cannot go in and possess the land until the rest of the Body is ready to go in with you."

I want to be ready to go! He told me I couldn't go until the rest of the Body was ready to go. It was at that moment that I became committed to the Body of Christ. I figured, if I can't go in alone and the Body has to go with me, then I'd better do my part to see everyone get ready because we're going in! I want to be like Caleb, even if I have to wait 40 years. Caleb said to Joshua after they had crossed over to the Promised Land, "Give me that land where we saw the giants. My strength has not abated. I'm stronger today than I was 40 years ago. Let me have those giants."

I get excited when I see these events coming to pass in light of the message of the Feasts and where we are in this generation. Everything that the Scripture tells us in terms of the events of the hour points out that this is the day the church will go into the land. **TO KEEP THESE FEASTS WILL CHALLENGE EVERY FIBRE OF YOUR BEING.**

To be the man or woman of God which the Word describes is not an easy task. It is something that you and I cannot attain outside of divine intervention in our life. It is not something that we can afford to fail to attain in this hour. We need the truth that is represented in these Feasts. We need to be the kind of Christians who will allow the Holy Spirit to bring its application in our lives and to deal with us. It's painful sometimes to be dealt with for our carnality, for our sinful attitudes, behavior and self-centeredness. God puts us in circumstances that bring out the weakness in our life. Because we can be strong in many ways in the Lord, sometimes those circumstances must be intense in order to bring a weakness out so it will surface, and in surfacing it can be yielded to the Lord and replaced by Him.

Keeping the Feast of the Day of Atonement is going to be a difficult experience. It is the most awesome and solemn day in the history of Israel. It is righteousness implemented; it is living the life, which means that we need to face the areas that we would like to sweep under the rug. It means that we have to allow God to deal with us in our relationships, especially our more interpersonal relationships where commitment, integrity, transparency, investment of self and self-denial find their fullest expression.

Once again, **the end of this process is the fullness of Christ formed in his people, so fully appropriating Calvary that we get a complete experiential victory over sin in terms of thought, deed and word. When we do, death will have no claim. Christ is coming in His fullness *IN* His people before He comes *FOR* His people.** Other generations have had their Joshuas and Calebs who believed for it, but because they weren't in the end-time generation they never experienced it. They have it as part of their inheritance to be granted to them at the time of rapture after the grave, but the Scriptures point out prophetically that a generation will arise which will bypass the grave, and it could be this one.

As we go through this study, it is my desire that you allow the Lord to stretch your concepts and that as a result, you will allow His dealings in your life to work with a greater intensity to fulfill His purposes.

Father, I recognize that this is a tremendous day in which to live, but I'm also very mindful of the fact that even during the time of your incarnation, there were multiplied thousands who missed their day of visitation. As you wept over Jerusalem, you cried, Oh Jerusalem, Oh Jerusalem, if only you'd heard me, I would have gathered you under my wings as a hen does her chicks. Lord, in this great day of opportunity, help us not to miss this day of visitation. Help us not to miss our opportunity. Father, we don't look at our own ability or desires to bring us to this fulfillment, but we're asking you to keep us. Lord, we commit this desire, we commit this goal, we commit this very important achievement into your hands, knowing that you are able to keep that which we commit to you against that day. Father, sensitize us, awaken us, motivate us to will and to do of your good pleasure. Work within us, break down every single resistance, root out bitterness and sinful attitudes and unbelief and things that hinder in order that we might be ready in the hour of visitation. Amen.

THE FEAST OF PASSOVER

The Passover period consisted of three celebrations, the first one called Passover, followed by the Feast of Unleavened Bread and Firstfruits. All of these took place within an eight-day period.

The memorial aspect of Passover is the event when Israel came up out of the nation of Egypt. It has a prophetic aspect which applies to Christ when He was our Passover Lamb. It also has an aspect that applies to us personally when we receive Christ.

And the Lord spoke to Moses and Aaron in the land of Egypt, saying, This month shall be unto you the beginning of months: it shall be the first month of the year to you. Speak unto all the congregation of Israel, saying, In the tenth day of this month they shall take to them every man a lamb, according to the house of their fathers, a lamb for a house. And if the household be too little for the lamb, let him and his neighbor next unto his house take it according to the number of the souls; every man according to his eating shall make your count for the lamb. Your lamb shall be without blemish, a male of the first year: ye shall take it out from the sheep, or from the goats: And you shall keep it up until the fourteenth day of the same month: and the whole assembly of the congregation of Israel shall kill it in the evening. And they shall take of the blood, and strike it on the two side posts and on the upper door post of the houses, wherein they shall eat it. Eat not of it raw, nor sodden at all with water, but roast with fire; his head with his legs, and with the purtenance thereof. And ye shall let nothing of it remain until the morning; and that which remaineth of it until the morning you shall burn with fire. And thus shall you eat it; with your loins girded, your shoes on your feet, and your staff in your hand; and you shall eat it in haste: it is the Lord's passover. For I will pass through the land of Egypt this night, and will smite all the firstborn in the land of Egypt, both man and beast; and against all the gods of Egypt I will execute judgment: I am the Lord. And the blood shall be to you for a token upon the houses where you are:

17

and when I see the blood, I will pass over you, and the plague shall not be upon you to destroy you, when I smite the land of Egypt. And this day shall be unto you for a memorial; and you shall keep it a feast to the Lord throughout your generations; you shall keep it a feast by an ordinance for ever. Ex. 12:1–14

For the Lord will pass through to smite the Egyptians; and when he sees the blood upon the lintel, and on the two side posts, the Lord will pass over the door, and will not suffer the destroyer to come in unto your houses to smite you. Ex. 12:23

The word "Passover" translated from the Hebrew and from the Greek has two kinds of meanings. One is literally "to go over the top of", and the other is to "hover over." In this picture we immediately see two things from God. We find that judgment or mercy will be according to faith and obedience, or unbelief and disobedience. Those who have faith in the provision of God and are obedient to that provision will find God's mercy. Those who do not find that connection with faith and obedience will reap the judgment of God. While judgment was taking place against the gods of Egypt and their people, the house of Israel was finding great deliverance and was being set free, but they had to partake in faith and obedience.

There are 19 points which I want to cover concerning the Passover:

1. **New Beginning.** "This will be the beginning of months for you; it shall be the first month of the year to you" (vs. 2). Israel is finding a beginning experience as a nation; it is the foundation of the entire covenant relationship that Israel as a people will have with God. When you have a beginning of months, then there is a sequel that follows, so all that is represented here by Passover is not an end. There are many Christians who have kept their Passover and that's as far as they've gone, not knowing or realizing that there is much more to do. We are expected to go on and keep the truths of the other feasts, but this is the beginning.

Its parallel is in II Corinthians 5:17, which says that if any man is in Christ, he is a new creation, old things pass away and all things become new. This is our foundation as Christians. Of course, we see the application to Christ: it was the beginning of a new creation, for He would be the firstborn of the new creation.

2. **The Lamb Was to be Set Aside for Four Days.** This has to do with the times and seasons of the Lord and with God's purposes. In the dispensations of God recorded in the Scripture, there are roughly 4,000 years from the time of the fall of Adam until the crucifixion of Christ. He was set aside from before the foundations of the world, and there was that time when He was set aside for four days and then brought to the altar of Calvary. We also see this picture on a different basis, for Luke 19:37 speaks of when Jesus entered Jerusalem during the Passion week:

> And when he was come nigh, even now at the descent of the mount of Olives, the whole multitude of the disciples began to rejoice and praise God with a loud voice for all the mighty works that they had seen.

This event was at the beginning of the Passover, on the 10th day of the month. On the 14th day, Christ was crucified. This was not by accident but was perfect fulfillment of Biblical typology.

The lamb set aside for four days speaks of divine purpose and timing. How this applies to us personally may be that before we come to Christ, it seems as though God has done a preliminary work in our spirit to bring us to a place where we are receptive to the message of the Gospel. It is in this time that we we are set apart for the day when we yield at the Cross of Calvary.

3. **It Was a Lamb of the First Year, the First Born.** The first born is interesting in that the first Adam brought sin and death into the world and, as a result, all of mankind was brought into bondage to Satan's kingdom. Jesus would come as the first born because He was going to make atonement. He would also be first born of a new creation because He would be the federal head of that new creation, as Adam was the federal head of the old creation.

4. Not only was it a lamb of the first year, but **it was to be a male.** Adam, as the federal head of the human race, would be the seed bearer of all unborn humanity. Every man, woman and child born into this world came from Adam's seed. Some ask, "What about the woman? She was the first one to break God's commandment." Yes, but she was made out of Adam and she was not the life-giver. The life-giver is the male. The Scripture teaches this all the way through and recently, in the study of genetics, it has been discovered that whenever a man

19

and woman come together and a child is conceived, the life component comes from the male contribution. In fact, the blood basically comes through the male contribution. That is what gives the life, and the Scriptures say the life is in the blood.

Adam was the first created, he was the federal head, in his loins was all of humanity and when he, as the federal head, fell, all that was within him fell. How does that work? The same way that we are suffering or being blessed by the decisions of our federal head in government. I Corinthians 15:22 says, "For as in Adam all die, even so in Christ shall all be made alive." The same principle by which all fell in Adam says that all can be made alive by receiving Christ.

5. This male had to be **without spot or blemish,** which deals with the perfection of the life of Christ.

> Forasmuch as you know that you were not redeemed with corruptible things, as silver and gold, from your vain conversation received by tradition from your fathers: but with the precious blood of Christ, as of a lamb without blemish and without spot: Who verily was foreordained before the foundation of the world, but was manifest in these last times for you.
> I Peter 1:18–20

You and I could never be the lamb; Christ has to be our Passover lamb. When Christ came to be sacrificed as our lamb, He came under inspection and there was no fault found in Him. I would like to spend a few minutes looking at those evidences in the Scripture. Some of the most obvious evidence comes from the testimony of Pilate, the highest Roman authority in the land at the time of the crucifixion of Jesus. His wife had been warned in a dream that he should not see this man crucified, and we read in John 18 about Pilate's inspection of Jesus:

> Then led they Jesus from Caiphas unto the hall of judgment: and it was early; and they themselves went not into the judgment hall, lest they should be defiled; but that they might eat the passover. John 18:28

> Pilate said unto him, What is truth? And when he had said this, he went out again unto the Jews, and said unto them, **I find in him no fault at all.** John 18:38

> Pilate therefore went forth again, and said unto them,

Behold, I bring him forth to you, that you may know that **I find no fault in him.** John 19:4

Then came Jesus forth, wearing the crown of thorns, and the purple robe. And Pilate said unto them, Behold the man! When the chief priests therefore and officers saw him, they cried out, saying, Crucify him, crucify him. Pilate said unto them, Take ye him, and crucify him: for **I find no fault in him.** John 19:5–6

We find that Herod makes the same testimony:

And when Herod saw Jesus, he was exceeding glad: for he was desirous to see him of a long season, because he had heard many things of him; and he hoped to have seen some miracle done by him. Then he questioned with him in many words; but he answered him nothing. And the chief priests and scribes stood and vehemently accused him. And Herod with his men of war set him at nought, and mocked him, and arrayed him in a gorgeous robe, and sent him again to Pilate. And the same day Pilate and Herod were made friends together; for before they were at enmity between themselves. Luke 23:8–12

Herod inspected Jesus but sent Him back to Pilate, the higher authority, *because he could not find anything in Jesus to condemn Him and he didn't want to have the responsibility.*

In John 18 there are a couple of other individuals who make a judgment upon Jesus: Annas and Caiphas, the high priests.

And they led him away to Annas first; for he was father in law to Caiphas, which was the high priest that same year. John 18:13

Annas had sent him bound unto Caiphas (vs. 24). If you've read the context, you find that they sent Him back and forth because *they could not find fault in Him.*

Now Caiphas was he, which gave counsel to the Jews, that it was expedient that one man should die for the people. John 18:24

There was a prophecy made that year by Caiphas, which appears in John 11:

And one of them, named Caiphas, being the high priest that same year, said unto them, Ye know nothing at all. Nor consider that it is expedient for us, that one man should die for the people, and that the whole nation perish not. And this spake he not of himself: but being high priest that year, he prophesied that Jesus should die for that nation; and not for that nation only, but that also he should gather together in one the children of God that were scattered abroad. John 11:49-52

The high priest then asked Jesus of his disciples, and of his doctrine. Jesus answered him, I spake openly to the world; I ever taught in the synagogue, and in the temple, where the Jews always resort; and in secret have I said nothing. Why are you asking me? Ask them which heard me, what I have said unto them: behold, they know what I said. And when he had thus spoken, one of the officers which stood by struck Jesus with the palm of his hand, saying, Answerest thou the high priest so? Jesus answered him, If I have spoken evil, bear witness of the evil: but if well, why smitest thou me? Now Annas had sent him bound unto Caiphas the high priest. John 18:19-24

And *they were not able to find evil in him.* Judas has his testimony: "I have sinned in that *I have betrayed the innocent blood*" (John 27:4).

When the centurion, and they that were with him, watching Jesus, saw the earthquake, and those things that were done, they feared greatly, saying. *Truly this was the Son of God.* Matt. 27:54

The repentant thief bore witness of Him: *"This man has done no evil.* We've done evil, we deserve to die, but this man *has done nothing wrong."*

HE WAS INSPECTED, AND NONE HAD CONVINCED OF SIN OR EVIL. HE WAS WITHOUT SPOT AND WITHOUT WRINKLE. What a beautiful picture that has been fulfilled!

6. **A Lamb for a House.** God has always dealt with houses, nations and a people. In the New Testament counterpart, we read this promise of God in Acts 16:15:

And when she was baptized, and her household, she besought us, saying, If you have judged me to be faithful to the Lord, come into my house, and abide there.

In verse 31, we find Paul and Silas in jail and the jailer was about to kill himself because they were escaping by God's intervention. The jailer asked how he could be saved, and Paul said, "Believe on the Lord Jesus Christ and thou shalt be saved and your house." The promise of God: a Lamb for a house.

Notice the typology in Exodus 12. The father caused the family to be obedient to him and to remain inside the house and to partake of the Passover; he applied the blood, and the whole household was protected. We have lost some of that today because many men do not manage their households anymore.

> And God is able to make all grace abound toward you;
> that you, always having all sufficiency in all things,
> may abound to every good work. II Cor. 9:8

Grace is part of this household provision and is something that is very important in the Passover. When people get saved, they don't realize that predicated upon the principles of keeping the Passover, if we will believe God and obey Him, He has given us a promise for the salvation of our house. Notice that it does not say they will be saved immediately, in the first week that you are a Christian. It doesn't say that they will become great people of faith and power. It simply says that THEY WILL BE PROTECTED BY THE BLOOD AND THAT THE DESTROYER WILL NOT ENTER IN.

7. **To be Killed in the Evening** (vs. 6). The marginal rendition says, "between the two evenings." This means they were to kill the lamb on the 14th day, between the two evenings. Jesus was crucified between 9:00 a.m. and 12:00 noon, between the two evenings.

Jesus' death is what saves us, then His life. Don't ever forget that. We appreciate the spotless, pure life of Christ and the fact that His life has been placed within us by the miracle of the new birth in order to have an overcoming power to live a life of righteousness, but we are first saved by His death.

> But God commends his love toward us, in that, while
> we were yet sinners, Christ died for us. Much more
> then, being now justified by his blood, we shall be
> saved from wrath through him. For if, when we were
> enemies, we were reconciled to God by the death of his
> Son, much more, being reconciled, we shall be saved
> by his life. Rom. 5:8–10

Notice the pattern. Death was necessary in order for

covenant relationship and the will of God to be carried out.

> And almost all things are by the law purged with blood; and without shedding of blood there is no remission. Heb. 9:22

In the Passover there must be a death, the penalty and wage for sin. Christ, the pure white Lamb, without spot or wrinkle, became our substitute.

8. **The whole assembly is to kill it** (vs. 6). This certainly finds its picture when Christ stood with Pilate on the veranda that day and they all cried out together en masse, "Crucify him, crucify him." Christ died because of you and because of me. We are guilty of the body and the blood of Jesus. Our sin put Him on the tree.

9. **The blood is to be applied** (vs. 7). It isn't enough to believe in it, to know about it, to even see it — it must be applied or it is of no value. The blood of the lamb was shed as a provision for every household, but the blood had to be applied before that provision would be of any value. Many people think it's enough that they believe in God, but it isn't. You must have the blood applied in your life.

> Whom God has set forth to be a propitiation through faith in his blood, to declare his righteousness for the remission of sins that are past, through the forbearance of God; to declare, I say, at this time his righteousness: that he might be just, and the justifier of him which believes in Jesus. Rom. 3:25–26

10. **All of the Flesh Must be Eaten** (vs. 8–10). It is to be roasted by fire, without water, which basically means that what happened at Calvary is never to be watered down. Roasted by fire speaks of the fires of judgment.

We find that it is to be eaten with unleavened bread, leaven being a type of sin and insincerity. A person can call on the name of the Lord for salvation without sincerity of heart and will receive nothing. You get about as much of God as you're willing to give of yourself. The Scripture says, "You shall seek me, and find me, when you shall search for me with all your heart" (Jer. 29:13). He is about as real with you as you are with Him.

The lamb is also to be eaten with bitter herbs. The bitterness is there because He would take the full bitterness of the Calvary experience and the judgment for our sins.

Christ died in purity and in sincerity, and we are to partake in this way.

> Jesus said unto them, Verily, verily, I say unto you, Except you eat the flesh of the Son of man, and drink his blood, you have no life in you. Whoso eats my flesh, and drinks my blood, has eternal life; and I will raise him up at the last day. For my flesh is meat indeed, and my blood is drink indeed. As the living Father has sent me, and I live by the Father: so he that eats me, even he shall live by me.
> John 6:53–55,57

What was Jesus saying? Are we all to become cannibalistic and try to find a piece of His flesh 2,000 years after He died? No, that's not what was being said. Who was Jesus? The Word. In the beginning was the Word, and the Word was with God, and the Word was God, and the Word became flesh and dwelt among us. Jesus said that by partaking of the Lamb, we would live by Him and by His life, just as He lived by the life of the Father. There are many people who sit down and watch Christianity go by. They hear about it, they observe it, but they never partake of it. It isn't enough to hear the Word, it isn't enough to hear about God, it's not enough to even observe God's supernatural intervention. WE MUST EAT OF THE LAMB AND PARTAKE OF HIS LIFE.

ONE WAY TO DO THIS IS BY PRAYER. Many people live their Christianity without communing with God. They read the Bible, they see what it says, they listen to what people say and they believe in it, but when it comes to personal interaction with Jesus Christ, they have very little because they have failed to partake of His life. If you don't have personal interaction with Jesus, then your Christianity is not Biblical and you haven't really kept the Passover. You must meet with Jesus personally because there is only one mediator between man and God, and that is the man Christ Jesus. You need to personally let God speak to your life, hear Him, acknowledge Him and let Him work in your life. You must personally reach out to Him, relate to Him and interact with Him. WE PARTAKE OF CHRIST BY KEEPING THE WORD. We don't love in word only but in deed and in truth. What you are speaks louder than anything you ever say. If you don't do His Word, then you don't love Him. Jesus said,

"If you love me, keep my commandments." BY DOING THE WORD, WE ARE BEGINNING TO PARTAKE OF HIM, AND AS WE PARTAKE OF HIM, WE WILL BEGIN TO GROW AND DEVELOP AND BEGIN TO KNOW HIM. IN KNOWING HIM WE WILL RELATE TO HIM.

11. **The Lamb Was to be Eaten in Haste** (vs. 11). Their loins were to be girded, their shoes on their feet, their staff (the sword of the Spirit) in their hand, and they should be ready to leave in haste. There is a parallel in Ephesians 6 in the statement concerning the Christian's armor in war:

> Stand therefore, having your loins girt about with truth, and having on the breastplate of righteousness. And your feet shod with the preparation of the gospel of peace. Eph. 6:14–15

Why in haste? On the following day they were going to march out of Egypt, never to return again. There was no longer any time for the believer to play around, just as there is no time for the Christian to play around in this world. We are pilgrims, translated out of the kingdom of darkness and into the Kingdom of His dear Son. We are citizens of another nation, ready to depart.

Keeping the Passover means that you cut off your relationships with the world which are outside of God's pattern in His Word, and you walk away clean. My friend Steve Fox is a good example. I know it wasn't easy for him to keep his Passover feast. I had the privilege of walking through the valley of decision with him after our crusade in Yokohama, Japan. He was the bass player for a group called Godigo which sold five gold records in 1979 and netted $72 million. He had fame and fortune, but he had come to really know Jesus. He witnessed in his concerts, but what he was and what he was doing were contradictory to his testimony. One day Steve decided he was ready to keep Passover fully — he was going to depart from Egypt. He knew he had to leave the band. Being the most popular one in the group, he also felt obligated to the other members because he felt the band would lose its fame. I remember talking two and-a-half hours long distance to Steve in Tokyo as he sobbed and cried and struggled. It was one of the hardest decisions that he's ever had to make, but he made it. He ate the Feast of Passover with haste and left Egypt.

We were privileged to be instrumental in helping Steve get established in a ministry training school for young people, according to the calling that God had placed on his life. At first it was like a wilderness for him. Since 1946 when World War II came to an end, it has been considered a very successful missionary who, after a year's effort, has won three or four people to Christ in Japan. Steve left Egypt and today is a missionary in Japan having unprecedented results for the Kingdom of God in that nation!

12. He Will Not Allow the Destroyer to Enter the Houses to Smite Them.

He that dwelleth in the secret place of the most High shall abide under the shadow of the Almighty. I will say of the Lord, He is my refuge and my fortress: my God; in him will I trust. Surely he shall deliver thee from the snare of the fowler, and from the noisome pestilence. He shall cover you with his feathers, and under his wings shall you trust: his truth shall be your shield and buckler. You shall not be afraid for the terror by night; nor for the arrow that flies by day; nor for the pestilence that walks in darkness; nor for the destruction that wasteth at noonday. A thousand shall fall at thy side, and ten thousand at thy right hand; but it shall not come nigh thee. Only with thine eyes shall you behold and see the reward of the wicked. Because you have made the Lord, which is my refuge, even the most High, thy habitation; there shall no evil befall thee, neither shall any plague come near thy dwelling. Ps. 91:1–10

That's a Passover promise to be appropriated by faith.

And they had a king over them, which is the angel of the bottomless pit, whose name in the Hebrew tongue is Abaddon, but in the Greek tongue has his name Apollyon ["destroyer"] (Rev. 9:11).

The thief comes not, but to steal, and to kill, and to destroy: I am come that they might have life, and that they might have it more abundantly. John 10:10

Forasmuch then as the children are partakers of flesh and blood, he also himself likewise took part of the same; that through death he might destroy him that had the power of death, that is, the devil. Heb. 2:14

27

It's quite clear who the destroyer is: the devil, Satan. He had the power of death in the Old Testament, but the scripture says in Hebrews that Jesus partook of flesh and blood that He might destroy him who had the power of death. The word "destroy" in the Greek means to render powerless. Between the fall and Christ's resurrection from the grave, Satan had the power of death on planet earth. But Christ took away from Satan the keys of death, hell and the grave. He had overcome the usurper and became once again the ruler of heaven and earth, and He is bringing back the rule of God on this planet.

This is a beautiful picture of the personal aspect of the covering presence of the Almighty due to His blood — perfect protection:

> And you shall take a bunch of hyssop, and dip it in the blood that is in the bason, and strike the lintel and the two side posts with the blood that is in the bason: and none of you shall go out at the door of his house until the morning. For the Lord will pass through to smite the Egyptians; and when he sees the blood upon the lintel, and on the two side posts, the Lord will pass over the door, and *will not suffer the destroyer to come in unto your house to smite you.* And you shall observe this thing for an ordinance to you and to your sons forever. Ex. 12:22–24

There was safety in the blood–bought multitude. It was tied to faith and it was conditional on their obedience. Even though they applied the blood, if they were disobedient to God's directive and left the house, they would be outside of God's safety. When we get outside of the Body of Christ, the household of God, and ignore the directives of God's delegated authorities in our life, we don't have any guarantee of this kind of protection. However, IF WE WILL WALK INSIDE THIS GOD–GIVEN PROVISION, HE HAS PROMISED THAT HE WILL NOT SUFFER OR ALLOW THE DESTROYER TO COME INTO OUR HOUSE TO SMITE US.

13. **This Was to be a Memorial** (vs. 14). Its parallel is the Lord's Supper, where the bread is broken and blessed when Jesus says, "This is my body which is broken for you"; He takes of the cup and says, "This is my blood in the new covenant shed for you. Do this as often as you eat or drink in remembrance of me."

14. **The Bones Are Not to be Broken.**

In one house shall it be eaten; thou shalt not carry forth ought of the flesh abroad out of the house; neither shall ye break a bone thereof. Ex. 12:46

Psalm 34:20 is a prophecy of the crucifixion of Christ, our Passover Lamb: "He keeps *all his bones: not one of them is broken.*" When Christ was crucified, they broke the legs of the others who were on crosses with Him that day. They didn't want them to be alive after dark because it would defile the further feasts of the Passover period, according to their particular customs. In order to speed death, their legs were broken, accelerating the internal hemorrhaging. When they came to Christ, they didn't break His bones because He was already dead.

15. **Spoil the Egyptians.** As these children of Israel began to come out of Egypt, look at the things they received:

And he called for Moses and Aaron by night, and said, Rise up and get you forth from among my people, both you and the children of Israel; and go, serve the Lord, as you have said. And take your flocks and your herds, as you have said, and be gone; and bless me also. And the Egyptians were urgent upon the people, that they might send them out of the land in haste; for they said, We be all dead men. And the people took their dough before it was leavened, their kneadingtroughs being bound up in their clothes upon their shoulders. And the children of Israel did according to the word of Moses; and they borrowed of the Egyptians jewels of silver, and jewels of gold, and raiment.

(The word "borrowed" here is a poor translation; it is "demanded" in the Hebrew.)

And the Lord gave the people favor in the sight of the Egyptians, so that they lent unto them such things as they required. And *they spoiled the Egyptians.*
Ex. 12:31–36

They had been slaves for 400 years and were getting their back wages!

Now the sojourning of the children of Israel, who dwelt in Egypt, was four hundred and thirty years. And it came to pass at the end of the four hundred and thirty years, even the selfsame day it came to pass, that all the hosts of the Lord went out from the land of Egypt.

It is a night to be much observed unto the Lord for bringing them out from the land of Egypt: this is that night of the Lord to be observed of all the children of Israel in their generations. Ex. 12:40–42

Out they went with the spoils of Egypt. What else happened at Passover?

He led captivity captive, and gave gifts unto men. Eph. 4:8

And you are complete in him, which is the head of all principality and power. Col. 2:10

[By Calvary] blotting out the handwriting of ordinances that was against us, which was contrary to us, and took it out of the way, nailing it to his cross. And having spoiled principalities and powers, he made a show of them openly, triumphing over them in it. Col. 2:14–15

Calvary brought to the church the spoils of victory over the ruling principalities and powers of darkness on planet earth.

16. **No Uncircumcised Males Were Allowed to Partake of the Passover** (vs. 43–51). We are not circumcised with the circumcision of the flesh but the circumcision of the heart, which means that we die to the natural man unto God. We must have become partakers of the new covenant relationship with the Lord. We cannot partake of the Lord's Supper if we haven't partaken of the Passover by being born again. "He that eats this bread and drinks this cup unworthily eats and drinks damnation unto himself, not discerning the Lord's body."

17. **Holy Convocation.** All of the feasts were considered sabbaths. The people were to do no work therein. The sabbath spoken of in Hebrews 4 teaches us what this is all about. We do have a sabbath day that we keep in the new covenant. It's not a Sunday or Saturday, although I believe in the principle of one day a week taught in the Scriptures. THE GENUINE MEANING OF THE SABBATH IS THAT WE CEASE FROM OUR OWN LABORS, WE CEASE FROM ADAM; WE ARE TO CEASE FROM LIVING BY AND ACTING IN OUR FALLEN ADAMIC NATURE AND ARE TO LIVE, ACT AND ABIDE IN THE LIFE OF CHRIST THAT IS IN OUR SPIRIT BY THE NEW BIRTH.

18. The healing power of God was manifested during this time:

He brought them forth also with silver and gold: and there was not one feeble person among their tribes.
Ps. 105:37

About three million people came out of Egypt. As slaves they had not had proper diets, nutrition or latrines; they had heavy work, probably beyond what would be healthy for most, many of them being old, and out of that crowd of three million there was not one feeble person among them.

Not only was that true then, but God intended it to be a continuing expression of keeping the Passover.

And there assembled at Jerusalem much people to keep the feast of unleavened bread in the second month, a very great congregation. And they arose and took away the altars that were in Jerusalem, and all the altars for incense took they away, and cast them into the brook Kidron. Then they killed the passover on the fourteenth day of the second month: and the priests and the Levites were ashamed, and sanctified themselves, and brought in the burnt offerings into the house of the Lord. And they stood in their place after their manner, according to the law of Moses the man of God: the priests sprinkled the blood, which they received of the hand of the Levites. For there were many in the congregation that were not sanctified: therefore the Levites had the charge of the killing of the passovers for every one that was not clean, to sanctify them unto the Lord. For a multitude of the people, even many of Ephraim, and Manasseh, Issachar, and Zebulun, had not cleansed themselves, yet did they eat the passover otherwise than it was written. But Hezekiah prayed for them, saying, The good Lord pardon every one that prepareth his heart to seek God, the Lord God of his fathers, though he be not cleansed according to the purification of the sanctuary. And the Lord hearkened to Hezekiah, *and healed the people.* II Chron. 30:13–20

In this passage we see how King Hezekiah was once again causing backslidden Israel to come back to the law, and as they kept the Passover, it talks about how they were healed. "And the Lord hearkened to Hezekiah, and healed the people." As they partook of the Passover as a memorial, the healing power of God was released amongst the sick and they received their healing. When we keep Passover, we find healing. It's part of what happened in the Atonement, and it is seen in Isaiah 53:3, "By his stripes we are healed." It is to be an on-going thing so that when we partake of the Lord's Supper as a memorial, those who partake of it in the faith of God will receive healing in their body.

19. **They Sang the Song of Moses** (Ex. 15), the first redemptive song ever sung in the Scripture. In Revelation 5:9-10 we read about the redeemed as they come home:

> And they sang a new song, saying, Thou art worthy to take the book, and to open the seals thereof: for thou wast slain, and hast redeemed us to God by thy blood out of every kindred, and tongue, and people, and nation: And hast made us unto our God kings and priests: and we shall reign on the earth.

Praise the Lord! No one but the redeemed can sing the song of redemption.

Father, we are so grateful for Jesus, our Passover Lamb. Through Him we have redemption, cleansing, healing, and wholeness in our families, protection from the enemy, deliverance from the bondage of sin, the spoils of Egypt, and a freedom to enter a new life as a new creation in Christ. As we keep the Passover Feast, let us remember to go on to all that you have planned and prepared for us. Amen.

THE FEAST OF UNLEAVENED BREAD

Many people have difficulty when they start looking into the New Testament from the Old. They say, "Well, let's throw out the Old Testament and keep the New." You can't, because the New is enfolded in the Old and the Old is enfolded in the New. They have different focuses in order to give a more balanced picture and understanding of the things of God. In fact, the entire New Testament was written as an unfolding of the Old, which many people don't understand. I want to give you a few things from the Scripture that will help you if you happen to be one of those who have difficulty looking at the Old Testament.

> And, behold, two of them went that same day to a village called Emmaus, which was from Jerusalem about threescore furlongs. Luke 24:13

They were walking along together and someone drew up near them. If you read the rest of the story, you know that person was Jesus. As He talked with them, He began to share the things of God. They didn't recognize Him, according to verse 16. This shows that Christ, even though He was resurrected and walking with the disciples, could not be seen and understood in the natural. We only receive the things of God by the Spirit of God. We go to verse 19:

> And he said unto them, What things? And they said unto him, Concerning Jesus of Nazareth, which was a prophet mighty in deed and word before God and all the people: And how the chief priests and our rulers delivered him to be condemned to death, and have crucified him. But we trusted that it had been he which should have redeemed Israel: and besides all this, today is the third day since these things were done.

The Old Testament at that point in time was the only source the early Christians had, but by the time we get into verse 44, we read this:

> And he said unto them, These are the words which I spake unto you, while I was yet with you, that all things must be fulfilled, which were written in the law of Moses, and the prophets, and in the psalms, concerning me. Then opened he their understanding,

that they might understand the scriptures.
Luke 24:44–45

That would have been an interesting Bible course! He basically outlined all of the things in the Old Testament speaking of Him, and we should understand what they are.

Repent ye therefore, and be converted, that your sins may be blotted out, when the times of refreshing shall come from the presence of the Lord: And he shall send Jesus Christ, which before was preached unto you: Whom the heaven must receive until the times of restitution of all things, which God hath spoken by the mouth of all his holy prophets since the world began. For Moses truly said unto the fathers, A prophet shall the Lord your God raise up unto you of your brethren, like unto me; him shall ye hear in all things whatsoever he shall say unto you. And it shall come to pass, that every soul, which will not hear that prophet, shall be destroyed from among the people. And all the prophets from Samuel and those that follow after, as many as have spoken, have likewise foretold of these days. Acts 3:19–24

The Scripture is full of these references, and we must recognize that it is a Biblical approach to look at the Old Testament and see Christ and the things concerning the church.

But their minds were blinded: for until this day remains the same veil untaken away in the reading of the old testament; which veil is done away in Christ. But even unto this day, when Moses is read, the veil is upon their heart. Nevertheless when it shall turn to the Lord, the veil shall be taken away. Now the Lord is that Spirit: and where the Spirit of the Lord is, there is liberty. But we all, with open face beholding as in a glass the glory of the Lord, are changed into the same image from glory to glory, even as by the Spirit of the Lord. II Cor. 3:14–18

People reading the Old Testament don't understand what it says until their heart is towards God and they come to Christ, because the veil is removed in Christ.

And on the fifteenth day of the same month is the feast of unleavened bread unto the Lord: seven days you

must eat unleavened bread. In the first day you shall have a holy convocation: you shall do no servile work therein. But you shall offer an offering made by fire unto the Lord seven days: in the seventh day is a holy convocation: you shall do no servile work therein. And the Lord spoke unto Moses, saying, Speak unto the children of Israel, and say unto them, When you come into the land which I give unto you, and shall reap the harvest thereof, then you shall bring a sheaf of the firstfruits of your harvest unto the priest.
Lev. 23:6-10

Unleavened Bread was followed by Firstfruits and was to go on for seven days. We will begin to understand the meaning of this feast by looking at its past memorial aspect –- what God did with Israel and Egypt. The original Unleavened Bread feast was to be kept in memory because of what God did and it would have prophetic significance for something God would do.

The **PAST MEMORIAL ASPECT** was their coming out of Egypt. On the night of the Passover they were to eat unleavened bread and were to be ready to move out of Egypt immediately to meet with God in the wilderness, where they journeyed for 50 days. They met God at Mt. Sinai, where He spoke to them audibly, and they entered into the law of covenant. The head of the house was exhorted to cleanse the house from all of the leaven for seven days after they arrived in the Promised Land. It was a memorial of the fact that they were delivered from their problems in Egypt and came out to enter into relationship with God.

The **PROPHETIC ASPECT** gets really exciting because this deals with some of the things that happened with Christ. I want to set a context for you as we begin. On the tenth day of the first month in the Jewish calendar, they were to take a lamb for the Passover feast and set it aside for four days. This was the day that Jesus entered Jerusalem and fulfilled the prophecy of Zechariah. There was tremendous praising before Him as He came into Jerusalem and was set aside for those four days. Passover was on the 14th day of the month, and as you go back to the lunar calendar in the year that Christ was crucified, you find that it happened to be on a Wednesday, contrary to tradition. He was crucified on the 14th, buried on the 15th, which was the day that Unleavened Bread began,

35

and rose on the day of the Feast of Firstfruits. He was in the heart of the earth for three days and three nights, according to the prophecy relating to Him as Jonah being three days and three nights in the belly of the whale.

> Then certain of the scribes and of the Pharisees answered, saying, Master, we would see a sign from thee. But he answered and said unto them, An evil and adulterous generation seeks after a sign; and there shall no sign be given to it, but the sign of the prophet Jonas: For as Jonas was three days and three nights in the whale's belly; so shall the Son of man be three days and three nights in the heart of the earth. Matt. 12:38–40

On the Jewish calendar, the day began in the evening; in other words, the evening and the morning were the first day (Gen. 1:5). If you were to number your days, Day One would begin this evening; tomorrow night after sundown would be the beginning of Day Two. Tradition has it that Christ was crucified on Friday, buried on Friday night and rose on Sunday. Christ was not crucified on Friday, but on a Wednesday afternoon. In John 19 we find the reason for the confusion. Christ was crucified on Passover, which was a sabbath; some have thought He was crucified on Friday night because that night is the beginning of Saturday, which is the beginning of the weekly sabbath.

> And it was the preparation of the passover, and about the sixth hour: and he said unto the Jews, Behold your King! John 19:14

That was Passover followed by a sabbath, which was the day of Unleavened Bread, a high day. Every one of these feasts begins with a sabbath. There were two sabbaths in the Passover week: the sabbath which began on Unleavened Bread and the normal sabbath day on Saturday. Leviticus 23:8 says that the first day of Unleavened Bread was a high day, a special sabbath.

> The Jews therefore, because it was the preparation, that the bodies should not remain upon the cross on the sabbath day, for that sabbath day was a high day, besought Pilate that their legs might be broken, and that they might be taken away. John 19:31

On that night, Wednesday, Jesus was brought down from the cross. That is actually the beginning of the 15th on the Jewish calendar, which was the beginning of the Feast of Unleavened Bread, so Unleavened Bread speaks of Christ's burial. He was buried on Thursday (our Wednesday night); three days later He rose and fulfilled the prophecy of Jonah. He rose then on the first day of the new week, which is Sunday. That is the historical fulfillment.

We begin our Christianity when we keep the Feast of Passover, when we kneel at Calvary and receive Christ and recognize that He died as our substitute. But that is not enough — we have to go beyond this beginning if we want all that God has provided. The next step is the Feast of Unleavened Bread.

For **THE PERSONAL ASPECT,** we must understand the concept that it is kept seven days. **Seven is always the number of completion in Scripture, so this speaks of a complete setting apart of one's life unto the Lord and to feed on Him for the rest of one's life. It is a complete commitment to Christ.** *Think of what that meant for Israel when they came up out of Egypt.* They kept the Feast of Unleavened Bread when they left Egypt, and when they left they had to leave 100%. When you come to Christ, if all you do is keep Passover and you don't keep Unleavened Bread, you will find that you will probably be dragged back into the world and struggle in your Christianity and end up falling away and being miserable. ONCE YOU HAVE SEEN THE LIGHT AND TASTED OF THE LIFE OF CHRIST, TO GO BACK INTO THE WORLD IS THE MOST TERRIBLE THING THAT CAN EVER HAPPEN TO YOU. YOU CAN'T EVEN ENJOY SIN ANYMORE! ONCE YOU HAVE HAD THE REALITY OF THE PLEASURES OF GOD AT HIS RIGHT HAND, THE IMITATIONS THIS WORLD HAS TO OFFER ARE SO FLAT, YOU HARDLY WANT TO EVEN GO THROUGH THE MOTIONS.

The Significance of Unleavened Bread in Israel: One way unleavened bread was used was in the consecration of the priests (Lev. 8:2,26). Whenever a priest was consecrated to serve, unleavened bread would be part of the ceremony. The Nazarite in Numbers 6:1-12 would make the vow of separation unto the Lord with unleavened bread. The meat offering and the peace offerings which were given with unleavened bread were food that the priests of the tabernacle would eat. Remember, you are a priest in Christ, and so it speaks of a spiritual sustenance that the Christian is to have. Unleavened bread was offered in every one of the feasts except Pentecost, which is very significant. It will help many of you from denominational backgrounds observing Pentecostals and Charismatics who have the Baptism of the Holy Spirit, speak with other tongues, have that anointing of God in their life and yet don't live like they should. That was already known about, understood and expected by God and was pictured by having leaven at the Feast of Pentecost.

Unleavened bread is symbolic of consecration and separation unto the Lord. It speaks of a total and complete consecration and commitment unto the Lord and a total breaking of our ties to the world. Unleavened bread was used when Gideon was called to serve in Judges 6:11–24 and was often involved when God sovereignly called one of His people into His service.

I once read an article in a Christian magazine about a person who is a dual citizen: a citizen in heaven and a citizen of America. I'm an American citizen, too. I take responsibility for my country as I believe we all should. I thank God for America, but I am not in America as just a citizen; I am here as a royal ambassador from the Kingdom of God! We must recognize that we are royalty and come out of the world. There is an identity change that must take place, and Unleavened Bread is part of it. God was saying, "You are no longer to be a part of Egypt, Israel; you are coming unto me to be a special people separated unto me and separated from the world." You are in the world, but that is not your source, it's not your home, it's not your country.

> Seven days shall ye eat unleavened bread; even the first day you shall put away leaven out of your houses: for whosoever eats leavened bread from the first day until the seventh day, that soul shall be cut off from Israel. Ex. 12:15

This is repeated in verse 19 and was a time of great cleansing. Leaven in the natural is something that you put in dough to ferment the whole lump, a means by which the bacteria makes the dough rot. It's corruption. A little leaven leavens the whole lump, the Scripture says. Spiritually, leaven in the Old Testament always spoke of that which must be put away from Israel's life. In the New Testament, it always speaks of that which is evil, either in doctrine or in practice. When we keep the Feast of Unleavened Bread, we are to get rid of everything that is evil in doctrine, in terms of our mind, in terms of our books, in terms of what we possess, and in terms of our behavior. This is done for seven days, the number of completion.

We find that Jesus died at Passover so that you and I might live. He dealt with the penalty of sin, which is death, but **He also dealt with the force and power of sin.** Passover gives us the cleansing of the blood, but we have to start a process by which we overcome the force and power of sin that has driven us, dominated us and destroyed us all our life. What is sin? One of my favorite Scriptures describing sin is, "He that knows to do good and does it not, to him it is sin." It doesn't mean that you did something wrong, but you failed to do what was right. Sin is also described as transgression of the law. In other words, **it is sin when we fall short of God's standard of love.**

In the New Testament there are five references to leaven. The first one is *the leaven of Herod.*

> And he charged them, saying, Take heed, beware of the leaven of the Pharisees, and of the leaven of Herod.
> Mark 8:15

Herod is the one spoken of in Mark 6:14–28.

> And king Herod heard of him; (for his name was spread abroad:) and he said, That John the Baptist was risen from the dead, and therefore mighty works do shew forth themselves in him. Others said, That it is Elias. And others said, That it is a prophet, or as one of the prophets. But when Herod heard thereof, he said, It is John, whom I beheaded: he is risen from the dead. For Herod himself had sent forth and laid hold upon John, and bound him in prison for Herodias' sake, his brother Philip's wife: for he had married her. For John had said unto Herod, It is not lawful for thee to have thy brother's wife. Therefore Herodias had a quarrel against him, and would have killed him; but she could not: For Herod feared John, knowing that he was a just man and an holy, and observed him; and when he heard him, he did many things, and heard him gladly. And when a convenient day was come, that Herod on his birthday made a supper to his lords, high

captains, and chief estates of Galilee; And when the daughter of the said Herodias came in, and danced, and pleased Herod and them that sat with him, the king said unto the damsel, Ask of me whatsoever thou wilt, and I will give it thee. And he sware unto her, Whatsoever thou shalt ask of me, I will give it thee, unto the half of my kingdom. And she went forth, and said unto her mother, What shall I ask? And she said, The head of John the Baptist. And she came in straightaway with haste unto the king, and asked, saying, I will that thou give me by and by in a charger the head of John the Baptist. And the king was exceeding sorry; yet for his oath's sake, and for their sakes which sat with him, he would not reject her. And immediately the king sent an executioner, and commanded his head to be brought: and he went and beheaded him in the prison. And brought his head in a charger, and gave it to the damsel: and the damsel gave it to her mother. Mark 6:14-28.

John the Baptist was filled with the Holy Spirit before he was born. He grew up in the wilderness and ate locusts and honey and wore a camel hair double–breasted suit and he didn't use the Madison Avenue technique. He set up his pulpit in the wilderness and God sent the people to him. One day John the Baptist made it into Jerusalem and started pointing his finger of righteousness and accusation toward the sin of Herod, and Herod put him in jail. He committed himself to killing John and even though Herod was afraid, John was beheaded. Jesus said, "Beware of the leaven of Herod."

That's the spirit of worldliness. It's like a fellow who had a baby boa constrictor. He would teach that snake how to wrap all around him and then unwrap. One day the trainer did something wrong and the snake was mad. The man gave the command to unwrap and the boa constrictor raised up his head, looked him right in the eye and began to squeeze until the man was squeezed to death.

Did you know that is the way sin is? That's the way worldliness is. You can play with it and it may be small for a while and seem harmless, but the day comes when it gets you. **Herod did not intend to kill John the Baptist, but he got caught by his lust, playing with worldliness, until one day he was destroyed by it.**

Another reference is *the leaven of the Saducees.*

> Then Jesus said unto them, Take heed and beware of the leaven of the Pharisees and of the Sadducees. And they reasoned among themselves, saying, It is because we have taken no bread ... How is it that you do not understand that I spoke it not to you concerning bread, that you should beware of the leaven of the Pharisees and the Sadducees? Then understood they how that he bade them not beware of the leaven of bread, but of the doctrine of the Pharisees and of the Sadducees. Matt. 16:6–12.

The Sadducees were a sect of the Jews who **did not believe in the supernatural;** they did not believe in spirit, angels or bodily resurrection. Today, that has its translation in what theologians call modernism. They want to explain everything in the Bible trying to use natural terminology because they don't believe in divine supernaturalism. They don't believe in demons, angels, spirits or the power of God. They don't believe in the resurrection and try to say it's all some hocus pocus that means something other than what it is.

The third reference to leaven is *the doctrine of the Pharisees* in the above passage and below.

> In the meantime, when there were gathered together an innumerable multitude of people, insomuch that they trode one upon another, he began to say unto his disciples first of all, Beware ye of the leaven of the Pharisees, which is hypocrisy. Luke 12:1

> All therefore whatsoever they bid you observe, that observe and do; but do not ye after their works; for they say, and do not. Matt. 23:3

Jesus was saying that what the Pharisees teach as far as doctrine is concerned is good, but they never practice what they preach. The word "hypocrite" comes from a word that was drawn out of the Greek theater. The theater would come out to act and would hold a little stick with a mask on the end of it in front of their face to help them act out the character. The name in the Greek language for that little mask was hupostatis, from which we get our word "hypocrisy": to wear a mask, **to pretend to be something that you are not. That's leaven.**

A fourth reference to leaven is:

> Your glorying is not good. Know ye not that a little leaven leavens the whole lump? Purge out therefore the old leaven, that ye may be a new lump, as you are unleavened. For even Christ our passover is sacrificed for us: Therefore let us keep the feast, not with old leaven, neither with the leaven of malice and wickedness; but with the unleavened bread of sincerity and truth. I Cor. 5:6-8

The Corinthians had all the gifts of the Spirit. The power of God flowed with them very beautifully, but they were full of sin. There was sensual sin, sexual sin, division, pride and egotism existing in that church. There is nothing wrong with miracles; God wants to perform them, but you should not glory in that fact when sin hasn't been purged from the camp. **These sins need to be dealt with and removed from your midst.**

> Know ye not that the unrighteous shall not inherit the kingdom of God? Be not deceived: neither fornicators, nor idolaters, nor adulterers, nor effeminate, nor abusers of themselves with mankind, nor thieves, nor covetous, nor drunkards, nor revilers, nor extortioners, shall inherit the kingdom of God.
> I Cor. 6:9-10

The fifth reference to leaven is, *"A little leaven leavens the whole lump"* (Gal. 5:9). These were Gentile believers. They had been saved, filled with the Holy Spirit, going on with God, and here come all these Jewish Christians who had a little bit of pride about their Jewishness, saying, "Now you Gentiles, if you really want to do it right, all of you fellows have to get circumcised; you have to go to church on the sabbath day; you have to go through certain ceremonial washings in order to really walk with God." The leaven here was **LEGALISM.** It was a mixture of law and grace, of flesh and spirit. Paul writes, "If any man or any angel comes to you with a gospel that is another gospel than the one we preached, let him be a curse." **This would be a gospel of an historical Christ, a religious concept dealing with forms, methods and rituals instead of focusing on a vital relationship with the living person of the resurrected Christ.** One is religion, one is Christianity; one is death, one is life. Wherefore, it says in I Timothy that there will be those who will be ever learning but never coming to the knowledge of the truth, having the form of godliness but denying the power thereof. From such turn away.

I know what it's like to go into churches which were at one time great bastions for the work of God. I know what it's like to go into what you hear of as being a great church which sent out missionaries and fathered wonderful churches around the world, but which somehow have fallen away from what they once were. Instead of having a church service, I feel like conducting a funeral. All of the life has gone. They have all the form on the outside, but on the inside there is no presence of God, no vital relationship with Jesus. That is the leaven of the Galatians.

Now when we talk of keeping the Feast of Unleavened Bread, we must recognize that we are to see all of these things removed from our life. **The Scripture speaks of them as a spirit of worldliness, false doctrines, hypocrisy, sensuality, fornication, legalism — flesh.**

This feast is to be kept in sincerity and in truth. Sincerity is commendable, but it just isn't enough. I can take you to India and into certain ashrams in the Himalayas and show you men who have given their lives for what they believe, men of tremendous intelligence who have laid down everything and have nothing because they are hungry for spiritual reality. They are searching and they are reaching, but they haven't found it. Sincere, yes, many of them showing a sincerity that would put many Christians to shame, but their sincerity isn't enough. They need truth. Did you ever have to write answers to little math problems on the board in grammar school? The teacher calls five of you to the board and says, "2 + 3," and you look at all of the answers. One has 4, another has 6, another 5. They're all convinced that they're right, they are all perfectly sincere, but two of them are sincerely wrong. We need sincerity and truth.

The sanctified life begins to take place with Unleavened Bread. This life is a continuing work. You keep the Feast of Unleavened Bread and there follows a working out of that sanctifying process of removing leaven from your life. How is that done?

Remember, **Calvary was a revelation of God's wrath against sin. You can't ever look at Calvary and not recognize that God will judge sin, for He judged His Son**

43

for your sin and mine. It's also a picture of God's love for us because He bore that wrath on our behalf. Jesus died for our sin but now we must see the power of sin broken. The old man is crucified with Christ (Rom. 6:6). This is really referring to Adam, to your fallen carnal nature. This is the meaning of Unleavened Bread — *the old man is dead* and you are to come out of him at Firstfruits and walk in newness of life! The reason this was written to the Romans was because of an old Roman concept. They would take a dead body and strap it to the back of a criminal and he would have to walk around with this dead body rotting on him. Eventually, the sick, rotten body would cause him to get disease and die. Why are you running around dragging your old man on your back? You don't have to serve sin any longer.

> I am crucified with Christ: nevertheless I live; yet not I, but Christ lives in me: and the life which I now live in the flesh I live by the faith of the Son of God, who loved me, and gave himself for me. Gal. 2:10

In other words, the old Roger Houtsma died at Calvary and the life energy that keeps me going is no longer the created life of Roger Houtsma. That life was crucified at Calvary and in its place I received the resurrected life of Christ. I live by His life, not through my faith but through the faith of the Son of God who loved me and gave Himself for me!

Romans 6:11 tells you how to think. If your thinking differs from God's Word, you need to adjust your thinking.

> Likewise reckon yourselves to be dead to sin, but alive unto God through Jesus Christ our Lord. Rom. 6:11

What does it mean to be dead? Go down to the morgue, pull out one of those drawers, take a big hat pin and poke that body and see what kind of reaction you get. That's what it means to be dead.

A boy asked a preacher what it means to be dead. The preacher said, "Go out to the graveyard and insult everybody." The boy went out and told everyone how ugly they were and how much they smelled, went back to the preacher and said, "I still don't know what it means to be dead." "Well, go back out there and flatter every one of them." "Hello, Mrs. Jones, you're so lovely today. Hello, Jack, you're really a handsome fellow." He came back to the preacher and said, "I still don't know what it means." "Well, what kind of a response did you

44

get?" "I didn't get any." "That's what it means to be dead." Dead to sin; *unresponsive to sin.* If someone insults you, are you unresponsive? Or does the old man rise up and say, "Why, just who do you think you are?" Or if they flatter you, how do you respond? "Well, I can see you have discernment!"

We are to be dead to sin, but alive to God. When the Spirit of God begins to move upon you, there is a responsiveness, a yielding, a recognizing and a longing after the Lord. That is how we are to reckon ourselves. When you do, I promise you that **THE HOLY SPIRIT WILL CAUSE YOUR EXPERIENCE TO BE MADE CONFORMABLE TO THE WORD.** You're battling in temptation, the old man starts to respond and get stimulated and excited with whatever the temptation is, and you know it's wrong. If you try to resist it by saying, "I won't do it, I won't do it, I won't do it," the next thing you know you will be doing it because **you will never get the victory by will power.** You don't have the strength in your natural man to overcome sin. Instead, if you call on the name of the Lord and say, "Jesus, I thank you that the old man was crucified in me at Calvary – **that means he's dead, I don't have to live under the power and bondage of that sin nature any longer, I'm free. I reckon myself as dead and unresponsive to that sin, and alive in response to your Spirit. Lord, I ask for your help right now,"** the Spirit of God will quicken you and all of a sudden the power of the temptation that was driving you inside will die. That's Unleavened Bread.

> Having therefore these promises, dearly beloved, let us cleanse ourselves from all filthiness of the flesh and spirit, perfecting holiness in the fear of God. II Cor. 7:1

We see this picture of holiness in water baptism, where the old man is buried and the new man comes forth, rising in newness of life. This is the meaning of Firstfruits, historically pictured in Israel coming out of Egypt, prophetically pictured in Christ's resurrection. Our personal result is finding ourselves animated by the new life of Christ on the inside, changing our motivations, our perceptions, our attitudes and our feelings, and we begin to walk in the life of the Spirit.

It is also pictured in the Lord's Supper. We are to keep the Lord's Supper on a regular basis; in so doing, we keep the Feast of Unleavened Bread. If we eat or drink of the Lord's Supper unworthily, not discerning the Lord's body, we will eat and drink damnation unto ourselves because we have not partaken with sincerity and truth but with leaven. It is to work as a cleansing agent for our life, because it is a point where once again we are brought to the Lord and say, "God, search my heart. Anything that is not right, I want to get straight right now. Cleanse me, forgive me. If it involves me getting reconciled with someone, I will do so." You can read about this in I Corinthians 10 and 11.

As we read in Psalms 105:37, there was not one feeble person among the Israelites coming up out of Egypt. THERE IS HEALING IN THE FEAST OF UNLEAVENED BREAD, FOR YOUR BODY AND FOR YOUR SPIRIT. Many people ask why the righteous suffer, why one person is healed and another isn't. I was with a person one day who was slowly dying of Alzheimer's Disease and who had been given two months to live. I spent the day sharing with that person, and a change started to come into his spirit. He had been carrying some bitterness for a number of years, justifying it, unwilling to go and be reconciled. He was a Christian seeking healing, filled with the Spirit, but not healed. I finally asked him, "Do you know why you're not healed? It's not that God wants to take you by disease. You're in this condition because you are now for the first time allowing God to deal with your spirit. You've had this disease for the last six years but for the last two months you've changed on the inside. God is changing your character for eternal things. You can't continue to go on and receive all of the blessings of God without allowing Him to clean you up. If you will allow God to really work that work on the inside and clean your spirit, He will create in your character His likeness and image. He will give you an abiding fruit, not just a moment of faith but abiding faith, not just a moment of joy but abiding joy, not just a moment of patience but abiding patience, not just a moment of self–control but an abiding fruit of self–control. If you allow the Spirit to do His work, this disease will never take you and God will raise you up out of that wheelchair and you will be healed by the power of the Holy Spirit." He recognized and received this immediately.

Healing didn't just come with Passover, it also came at the Feast of Unleavened Bread. When you start being insincere and allow this leaven to work in your life, some form of hypocrisy or whatever, you hinder receiving that healing. In fact, scripture warns us in the Corinthian epistle concerning the Lord's Supper that some were sick and some had died before their time because they had eaten and drunk of the Lord's Supper unworthily. They did so with insincerity and they did so with falsehood. As a result, God allowed sickness to come upon them and did not heal them. That does not mean that everyone who is sick is going through this problem, but it is true for some.

Why is one person healed and another is not? God sometimes heals out of mercy, He sometimes heals out of signs, but once we become Christians and start to walk with Him, He expects something from us. He wants us to allow His Spirit to work in us, to make us into His likeness and image, and if we don't allow His Spirit to do that, we may forfeit some of the benefits of Calvary. When I get sick, I always ask God, "All right, God, what are you after? Is there something in my life that has to go today?" Either the devil is attacking me (and if he is I don't have to put up with it) or the Lord is allowing it as a chastening point in my life to deal with me in order that I might change. If so, I want Him to get it over with quickly. Another reason I can get sick or afflicted is if I misuse my body.

What about long–term diseases? God has a point in everyone's life that becomes His scalpel, to shape us and to form us. Sometimes it's a husband, wife or child, sometimes it's a business or a desire and ambition, sometimes it's a sickness. **GOD'S NUMBER ONE PRIORITY IS TO MAKE YOUR CHARACTER INTO HIS LIKENESS AND IMAGE.** When you have a situation that God repeatedly uses in your life to deal with you, then you know that it is to be His scalpel. In order to have a continuing victory in that area one has to be continually pliable in His hands.

This is different than suffering for Christ. Did you ever wonder why Paul, preaching with Silas and Barnabas, was the only one stoned and left for dead? What about the others who were standing right there with him preaching the same thing?

Why was it that Peter was sifted as wheat by Satan on the night of Jesus' trial? Why not James or John? God knew that Peter needed to fail in order to break from his independence and to learn how to rely on the Lord for his source.

John needed to be dealt with. He was the one who said about the Samaritans, "Well, they didn't receive you, Lord

Jesus. Why don't we call fire down on them?" John came out as the apostle of love, the most gentle of all the apostles. It wasn't in his nature — God did it. John never failed as Peter did because that wasn't the means by which he would be changed.

There is a uniqueness in each of us, and as we yield to God's dealings to change us, then those points by which He gets our attention begin to be positive instead of negative and we find our way to victory in and over the circumstance. When we wrestle with Him and don't allow Him to change our spirit, then He just cranks the vise a little tighter until we say "uncle" and surrender. You don't want to wrestle with the Lord too much because He's going to win!

For Israel, keeping the feast would mean a complete separation from Egypt's gods, from Egypt's religion, from their bondage and slavery, from their food and from their work in Egypt, as well as the glory and the power and the might of the most powerful nation of their day. For the church, it speaks of the practical separation from all known evil and all of the corrupting influences in the life of the believer. We are to keep it as they kept it.

> And they baked unleavened cakes of the dough which they brought forth out of Egypt, for it was not leavened; because they were thrust out of Egypt, and could not tarry, neither had they prepared for themselves any victual. Ex. 12:39

They left quickly. You keep the feast by breaking away from the world — don't dilly-dally, don't play with leaven. Be like Joseph when he had to flee from Potiphar's wife. Flee fornication, flee youthful lust, flee doctrines of devils, flee these things and go on with God. John 6 says that Jesus is the bread of life that comes down from heaven. Christ was the only true pure one; press on to meet with Him and feed on His life.

Father, help us to open our hearts to the working of your Holy Spirit in cleansing us from all the leaven in our lives. Work in us to motivate us to quickly and fully break from our involvements with the spirit of the world so that, having come out, we will be free to enter in to all that you have intended in our lives. Amen.

THE FEAST OF FIRSTFRUITS

And the Lord spoke unto Moses, saying, Speak unto the children of Israel, and say unto them, When ye be come into the land which I give unto you, and shall reap the harvest thereof, then ye shall bring a sheaf of the firstfruits of your harvest unto the priest: And he shall wave the sheaf before the Lord, to be accepted for you: on the morrow after the sabbath the priest shall wave it. And ye shall offer that day when ye wave the sheaf a he lamb without blemish of the first year for a burnt offering unto the Lord. And the meat offering thereof shall be two tenth deals of fine flour mingled with oil, an offering made by fire unto the Lord for a sweet savour: and the drink offering thereof shall be of wine, the fourth part of an hin. And ye shall eat neither bread, nor parched corn, nor green ears, until the selfsame day that he have brought an offering unto your God: it shall be a statute for ever throughout your generations in all your dwellings. Lev. 23:11-14

But now is Christ risen from the dead, and become the firstfruits of them that slept. For since by man came death, by man came also the resurrection of the dead. For as in Adam all die, even so in Christ shall all be made alive. But every man in his own order: Christ the firstfruits; afterward they that are Christ's at his coming. I Cor. 15:20-23

This passage shows that **the resurrection of Christ is the prophetic fulfillment of the meaning of Firstfruits.** This feast came only when Israel entered into the promised land. It was not something they enjoyed when they came out of the nation of Egypt during the Passover. It was held on the third day, the very day on which Christ was resurrected.

It is a harvest feast and speaks of feeding on the fruit of the land. As you understand the meaning of this feast, you will know why it was not instituted in coming out of Egypt and in the wilderness but had to wait until they came into Canaan. In the wilderness, the Israelites ate of the manna daily supplied by God. When they entered into the promised land, they ate of the fruit of the land. This speaks to the church of a walk with God after having received Christ as Lord and Saviour.

Historically, we see where this feast was instituted in the Book of Joshua:

> And the manna ceased on the morrow after they had eaten of the old corn of the land; neither had the children of Israel manna any more; but they did eat of the fruit of the land of Canaan that year. Josh. 5:12

As soon as the Israelites entered the promised land and got somewhat established there, they began to eat of the fruit of the land and the supernatural supply of manna ceased. It was then that the Feast of Firstfruits was instituted.

What happened when Israel kept the Feast of Firstfruits under the old covenant? The winter barley and wheat that was sown would grow as it was watered by the winter rains, usually reaching maturity sometime in June. However, it would be around April when this feast was held, and the grain stalks would be standing in the field. The priests would take a sheaf of the standing stalk and bring it to the temple, where it was waved before the Lord on the day after the sabbath.

This sheaf pictures Jesus Christ as the first–born of the dead. He was resurrected on Firstfruits, **the prophetic fulfillment,** and being the first–born, there were many things that belonged to Him. Under the concept of firstfruits, the first–born animals were to be sanctified to God; the first–born child was to be sanctified and presented to the Lord; and our tithes and offerings are to come off of the top, the firstfruits, and brought to the Lord. The first–born who was sanctified unto God under the law had three major blessings belonging to him that the other children did not possess:

1. **RULING AUTHORITY** – He was to become the head in that family next to the father. As he reached maturity, he would share in the father's responsibilities and would have a ruling authority in the family.

2. **DOUBLE PORTION** – He would get a double portion of the inheritance. If there were three children, the first–born would get half of the estate and the other two children would each get a quarter thereof. Of course, the first–born had responsibilities. If something happened to his brothers or sisters, as the ruling sibling he would have the responsibility before God to take care of them.

3. **PRIESTLY SERVICE** – He would be called for priestly service.

Of the 12 children of Jacob comprising the fathers of the 12 tribes, we find that these three blessings went to three different children instead of to the first-born, Reuben. Reuben slept with one of Jacob's wives. As a result, **God judged him for his sin and he lost the birthright. The blessing of the birthright went three ways, and Joseph got the double portion. When you trace the tribe of Joseph, you find his two sons, Manasseh and Ephraim, are the ones who carry the blessing which would have been Reuben's. The kingly authority belonged to the tribe of Judah, out of which Christ would be born and rule. The priestly ministry went to the tribe of Levi.**

Christ, being the first-born of Mary, carried these three mantles on Him as the Son of Man, and when He was risen from the dead, He was the first of those resurrected. There are many who have been raised from the dead but not resurrected. When you're raised from the dead, your body is still corruptible; when you're resurrected from the dead, you have an incorruptible body.

As a new creation in Christ, as we partake of Him and keep the Feast of Firstfruits, we are to walk in newness of life without the encumbering bondages of the Adamic nature and the life born after the flesh. This is the **personal aspect. The sheaf of firstfruits needs to be distinguished from the harvest of firstfruits. The sheaves waved before the Lord in April were not yet mature,** which is an important aspect of this feast. The maturity time would come during the season of Pentecost, 50 days later, which meant that **the firstfruits offering was a promise of a harvest to come. It was a forerunner, a sample of what that coming harvest would be.** We see this when Christ was crucified:

> And, behold, the veil of the temple was rent in two from the top to the bottom; and the earth did quake, and the rocks rent; and the graves were opened; and many bodies of the saints which slept arose. And came out of the graves after his resurrection, and went into the holy city, and appeared unto many.
> Matt. 27:51-53.

That was the firstfruits offering. They were raised from the dead and were taken with Christ when He ascended into heaven, but *it was a promise of a much greater harvest to come.* Those who don't believe in the resurrection of the saints and the coming of the Lord have a hard time explaining this, because it is a foretaste of the promise of the resurrection of the saints. You and I are going to be resurrected at the coming of the Lord, unless we are alive when He comes and we bypass the grave.

> Of his own will begat he us with the word of truth, that we should be a kind of firstfruits of his creatures. James 1:18 And not only they, but ourselves also, which have the firstfruits of the Spirit, even we ourselves groan within ourselves, waiting for the adoption, to wit, the redemption of our body.
> Rom. 8:23

A harvest of resurrected saints took place with Jesus' resurrection, which was a kind of firstfruits, meaning **that there was a greater harvest to come.** The harvest which would follow was Pentecost. The priests took the sheaf, a picture of what was coming, and waved it before the Lord in the temple that it might be accepted for you. *The wave offering speaks of Christ's ascension to the heavenly tabernacle.* When Jesus rose from the dead, Mary Magdalene had gone to the grave along with other women to anoint His body. He was gone, He was resurrected. The other women left and Mary ran into a man whom she didn't recognize. When He spoke to her and said, "Mary," she recognized His voice and fell at His feet and said, "Rabboni, Master." He was not recognizable in His resurrected body, yet He was physical and looked human. Jesus said in John 20:17, "Don't touch me for I am not yet glorified," meaning that He had not yet ascended to the heavenly tabernacle with the Father. Later that day, Jesus was waved (presented) and accepted before God in our behalf. We had been separated from God because of sin, Jesus died for us and gave us the blood covering. The old man is separated in Unleavened Bread and in Firstfruits we rise in newness of life. And we find this, **His life, is waved for us as a Firstfruits and a sample of what shall be thereafter.** In other words, **we are the fruits that shall follow after to be found in His likeness and image.** Ephesians 1:6 says that you are accepted in the beloved. This means that **as a result of the Firstfruits offering and our experience of keeping that feast to walk in newness of life in a progressive process of sanctification, we have a standing before God that is as the standing of the Lord Jesus Christ.**

Notice that in this feast no sin offering was given. The reason for this is that **Christ is sinless, which is why death could not hold Him.**

In this beautiful acceptance which we have in the beloved and with its forecasting of a greater harvest, we already see a degree of what is to come. It is already pictured to an extent in that Christ was accepted for us and we are accepted in Him; He was the firstfruits and the firstfruits is a picture of what is to come; it is a promise and a prophecy that we will be found in His likeness and image.

> For whom he did foreknow, he also did predestinate to be conformed to the image of his Son, that he might be the firstborn among many brethren. Rom. 8:29

This doesn't mean you will look like Jesus. This speaks of character, the inner man having the traits and qualities of Jesus' character.

Jesus was the firstfruits of the first resurrection:

> And I saw an angel come down from heaven, having the key of the bottomless pit and a great chain in his hand. And he laid hold on the dragon, that old serpent, which is the Devil, and Satan, and bound him a thousand years. And cast him into the bottomless pit, and shut him up, and set a seal upon him, that he should deceive the nations no more, till the thousand years should be fulfilled: and after that he must be loosed a little season. And I saw thrones, and they sat upon them, and judgment was given unto them: and I saw the souls of them that were beheaded for the witness of Jesus, and for the word of God, and which had not worshipped the beast, neither his image, neither had received his mark upon their foreheads, or in their hands; and they lived and reigned with Christ a thousand years. But the rest of the dead lived not again until the thousand years were finished. This is the first resurrection. Blessed and holy is he that hath part in the first resurrection: on such the second death hath no power, but they shall be priests of God and of Christ, and shall reign with him a thousand years. Rev. 20:1–6

The first resurrection consists of all those who are born again believers in Christ; all of those in the Old Testament who believed in the prophecies of the Messiah; all of those after the rapture of the church who are saved during the Tribulation. These are all participants in the first resurrection.

In addition, Paul said, "Last of all he was seen of men also, as of one born out of due time" (I Cor. 15:8). God uses Paul also as a type of firstfruits by giving him as an example of what we are to be. Sometimes you will find a stock of wheat or barley in a field that rises up above the others and becomes ripe before its time while the major harvest is not going to be ripe for about six weeks. This is called a firstfruit. God uses Paul in this way, picturing a maturity to come for the body of Christ. "Be ye followers of me, even as I also am of Christ" (I Cor. 11:1).

Father, thank you for receiving Christ in our behalf and for the promise of His pure life as an example of what we shall be. Help us and teach us how to grow and to mature into the likeness and image of Christ. Cause us to walk more and more in your light and life unto the perfect day. Amen.

THE FEAST OF PENTECOST

Pentecost is a very exciting feast; it also has come to pass and is available to all today.

> Three times in a year shall all thy males appear before the Lord thy God in the place which he shall choose; in the feast of unleavened bread, and in the feast of weeks [Pentecost], and in the feast of tabernacles: and they shall not appear before the Lord empty: Every man shall give as he is able, according to the blessing of the Lord thy God which he hath given thee.
> Deut. 16:16

In keeping each of these feasts, the people were to come before God with something to give to Him. Learn this important principle about worship. Many people want to worship God but they don't understand that in order to worship, there is an element of sacrifice: you must have something to give. In every approach to God in the Old Testament one always had to bring an offering, and every one of those offerings cost something in the natural. They couldn't sacrifice a lamb without buying the lamb; they couldn't sacrifice a bullock without buying a bullock; they couldn't sacrifice a pigeon without buying a pigeon; they couldn't give a meal offering without making the cakes. It cost them something.

As a counterpart in the New Testament, we have three kinds of sacrifices: one is the sacrifice of praise, which is the fruit of our lips; another is to present our body before Him a living sacrifice; and the third one is to give out of our finance. If you are going to worship God, you must be involved with these sacrificial elements.

The Israelites came before the Lord three times in the year: once was Passover when they had Passover, Unleavened Bread and Firstfruits. The second time, 50 days after Firstfruits, was the Day of Pentecost when they were all to gather and worship the Lord.

> Three times thou shalt keep a feast unto me in the year. Thou shalt keep the feast of unleavened bread: And the feast of harvest [Pentecost], the firstfruits of thy labours, which thou hast sown in the field; and the feast of ingathering [tabernacles], which is in the end of the year, when thou have gathered in thy labours

out of the field. Three times in the year all thy males shall appear before the Lord God.

Ex. 23:14,15a,16-17

The firstfruits feast was a picture of the harvest to come, and Pentecost was when that harvest was reaped. A later harvest then would come in the fall. This Feast of Pentecost is the one that Moses referred to when he spoke to Pharaoh and said, "It is time for my people to come out of Egypt and go into the wilderness to have a feast with me." It was promised by Firstfruits.

The winter harvest is a promise, then, of a greater harvest to come. Once again, Firstfruits was not a harvest; it was a promise of Pentecost, the harvest to come at the beginning of the summer. Pentecost was a harvest of barley, wheat and grain. The harvest at the end of the summer was the harvest of fruit, and **a greater harvest came at the end of summer than at the end of winter.**

My brother–in–law is a farmer, and I remember going up around June to visit the family. They had been reaping the wheat and had the winter crop in. At the same time, we found a couple of branches from their fruit trees sitting in the living room. They had all been pollinated and the little buds of fruit were coming at the time the harvest of grain was taking place, so the buds of the fruit tree harvest were there also, almost like a firstfruit promise of another and even greater harvest to come. *That harvest of fruit is part of what makes Pentecost meaningful.* **PENTECOST LOSES ITS MEANING IF THERE IS NO HARVEST THAT FOLLOWS.**

There are two kinds of harvest that Christians can have: one is the harvest of souls brought into the Kingdom of God. Since the Pentecostal revival began at the beginning of this century, we have seen the greatest missionary activity and harvest of souls since the early church. **The other harvest is the fruit of the Spirit in our life — Christian character.**

Every new step with God carries a stigma with it. In the days of the early church, a believer would not have gone down to the local craftsman and have him make a little cross to put on a chain and wear it around his neck. Today, the cross is a decoration, but in that day it was a terrible stigma. Under the Roman rule, the worst death that they ever gave the vilest of criminals was crucifixion, and *the fact that Christ, the Son of*

God, was crucified was a stigma. It was such a strong stigma that one did not embrace it to gain the approval of men or to gain some blessing for himself. How many people who come to Christ today are into "what can I get out of it?" In the early church, they received persecution.

Every new step with God carries a stigma with it. It is often part of the pricetag for something more in God. To get the "want to" written in your heart, to get the fire of the Spirit that you might become a witness, to have the inner working of the Spirit, there is a price to pay. "After that the Holy Spirit comes upon you, you shall receive power, or divine enablement, and you shall become my witnesses." The Greek word for "witness" is "martos". The purpose of the Baptism of the Holy Spirit is for you to become a living martyr whereby the Holy Spirit will take the Cross of Jesus Christ and apply it to you, and your old man will be made to die that the life of Jesus might be manifest in you. People say, "Oh, I want the power." If you want the power, pay the price. "I want the blessing." Pay the price. The Scripture says that if you draw near unto God, He will draw near unto you. Jesus said, "If any man comes unto me, I will in no wise cast him out." The Scripture says, "He who comes to God must believe that he is and that he is a rewarder of those who diligently seek him." *If you want that reality with Him, you have to pay the price.*

There is a stigma with Pentecost: it is speaking in other tongues. The stigma keeps the insincere away because they don't want to bear the reproach of Jesus Christ.

It was a stigma for Jesus to walk amongst the people of Israel. He said, "Hitherto I work and my Father works," and they said, "You blasphemed." It was a stigma for Him to speak to a man with palsy and say, "Thy sins be forgiven," and they said, "Only God can do that; you've made yourself equal with God."

The stigma of Pentecost is being lost today. We have truth today for which many people have paid a terrible price. There are people in our congregation who, because they decided to follow the Lord and found reality with God, are being rejected by their families with other religious backgrounds. And that's nothing. In the early days of the Pentecostal Revival, you would leave a service and find your tires slashed and windows broken and rocks thrown against the building. Recently we had the Charismatic Renewal and everyone has a relative in it, so it's not quite as stigmatic! **Do you know why it's not such a stigma today? Because Pentecost is not the feast season of this hour. God has moved beyond Pentecost.**

Anointing for Service

And thou shalt anoint Aaron and his sons, and consecrate them, that they may minister unto me in the priest's office. And thou shalt speak unto the children of Israel, saying, This shall be a holy anointing oil unto me throughout your generations. Upon man's flesh shall it not be poured, neither shall ye make any other like it, after the composition of it: it is holy, and it shall be holy unto you. Ex. 30:30–32

The anointing oil comes with the Holy Spirit: you shall receive power, you shall receive the anointing after that the Holy Ghost has come upon you. This is not the end of the progressive anointing from God, but it is an important step.

Being baptized with the Holy Spirit with the evidence of speaking in other tongues is foundational. If you don't speak with tongues and you think it's all right, let me say this: In the Book of Acts, they all received the Baptism with the evidence of speaking in other tongues, and you've come up short of what they had in the early church if you don't speak in tongues.

Tongues is only the initial evidence; the secondary evidence is trouble! Immediately the Holy Spirit goes to work on you to bring every area of your life into submission to the Lordship of Jesus Christ, because Pentecost carries a promise of a greater fruit, Christian character. That means He is going to go to work on the areas of rebellion, stubbornness and sin in your life. Believe me, that's trouble — but He always wins. Sooner or later you learn to relax in His dealings and let the Lord have His way without fighting Him so much. I love what one brother said: "When I got saved and filled with the Holy Spirit, I was going all the way with the Lord, right to the Promised Land. I wasn't going to be like the children of Israel, wandering around in the wilderness for 38 years. I just saw my tracks through the desert going in a straight line right to the Promised Land. Then the next thing you know, I went out there, looked at my tracks and saw these heel marks going all the way across the desert." He had been resisting even though he didn't want to.

In the Book of Acts, the first two things a convert did after being saved was get baptized in water and filled with the Holy Spirit. You cannot really go on to keep Trumpets, the Day of Atonement and the Feast of Booths unless you go this far. Many people have kept the Feast of Passover without keeping Unleavened Bread and Firstfruits. Others have kept Passover, Unleavened Bread and Firstfruits but they have never kept Pentecost. These are all saved and part of the family, but there are certain things that are not realized in them because they haven't gone far enough.

Every believer needs to keep each one of these feasts. If you find you are missing in one of these areas, go back and take care of it. There has to come a time when we say, "All right, Lord, I'm at a place where I am no longer going to just react to you or to a situation, but I'm going to recognize that you're after something in my life. I'm going to make a conscious, disciplined effort to deal with the areas of need and to grow and mature and understand your answers and purposes and ways in my life." We need to make that kind of commitment to the Lord.

Worship

> And the priest shall wave them with the bread of the firstfruits for a wave offering before the Lord, with two lambs: they shall be holy to the Lord for the priest.
> Lev. 23:20

This is a sin offering and is symbolic of worship, something that happens with the Baptism of the Holy Spirit. It releases us to worship in Spirit and in truth. That's why we sing in tongues, clap our hands, raise our hands and wait in silence — all of the different ways that God gives us in the Word. We must learn to be worshippers, for the Father seeks for such who will worship Him in Spirit and in truth. **If you aren't a worshipper, you will never enter into God's fullness.** God wants you to be a worshipper, and you can begin by worshipping according to the truth of the Word in sincerity of heart. Out of true worship comes relationship, which leads to ministry.

A Feast of Rest

> And you shall proclaim on the selfsame day that it be a holy convocation unto you: ye shall do no servile work therein: it shall be a statute for ever in all your dwellings throughout your generations. Lev. 23:21

Our work hinders His work. We are to cease from our own ways to walk in His ways. When we do that at Pentecost, then we begin to enter into relationship. We will see later that Pentecost was really the formation of the church, just as at Sinai it was the formation of Israel as a nation under covenant with God. By one Spirit we all have access to the same Father; we're all born of Him, we're all part of the same family. You don't choose your brothers and sisters, but God says, "love them." There needs to be a formation of family relationship. There is to be a union of life — you and God and, as a result, you and everyone else who has a relationship with Him in the Spirit. You say, "I don't want to because I've seen sin in the church." The Feast of Pentecost is the one feast with leaven in it. God is telling us He knew there would be sin and He has already made a provision for it.

Truth shared is to be participated in and experienced. **We teach about salvation to get saved; we teach about healing to get healed; we teach about water baptism to be water baptized; we teach about the Feast of Pentecost and all of these other feasts so we can make sure that these truths are completely embraced. WE MAY HAVE KEPT SOME OF THESE FEASTS ONLY IN PART, BUT BECAUSE THEY ARE PREREQUISITES TO WHAT GOD IS DOING TODAY AND WHERE HE IS TAKING US IN THIS HOUR, GET THIS ACCOMPLISHED IN YOUR LIFE SO YOU CAN GO ON WITH WHAT GOD IS DOING TODAY. GOD HAS CHOSEN THIS GENERATION TO BE THE ONE THAT WILL HAVE THE GREATEST OPPORTUNITIES OF ANY PEOPLE WHO HAVE EVER GRACED THE FACE OF THE EARTH. WE ARE COMING TO COMPLETION.**

Application

One of the reasons the Pentecostal church lost the power it once had and the Feast of Pentecost began to lose its meaning is because the fruit that was promised thereafter was not experienced. The church did not go on to keep the Feast of Tabernacles. As stated before, the fruit of the Christian consists of the fruit of the Spirit, which is character, and the fruit of lost souls being brought into the Kingdom of God. We recognize that not only was Israel formed as a nation in the original Pentecost at Sinai, but at the day of Pentecost in the New Testament we find the formation of the Body of Christ.

You shall bring out of your habitations two wave loaves of two tenth deals: they shall be of fine flour; they shall be baked with leaven; they are the firstfruits unto the Lord. Lev. 23:17

Also in the day of the firstfruits, when you bring a new meat offering unto the Lord, after your weeks be out, ye shall have a holy convocation: you shall do no servile work: But you shall offer the burnt offering for a sweet savour unto the Lord; two young bullocks, one ram, seven lambs of the first year; and their meat offering of flour mingled with oil, three tenth deals unto one bullock, two tenth deals unto one ram, a several tenth deal unto one lamb, throughout the seven lambs; and one kid of the goats, to make an atonement for you. You shall offer them beside the continual burnt offering, and his meat offering (they shall be unto you without blemish) and their drink offerings. Num. 28:26–31

There are New Testament counterparts:

For we being many are one bread, and one body: for we are all partakers of that one bread. I Cor. 10:17

For he is our peace, who has made both one, and has broken down the middle wall of partition between us; having abolished in his flesh the enmity, even the law of commandments contained in ordinances; for to make in himself of twain one new man, so making peace. Eph. 2:14–15

One of the rituals done on this particular feast day, along with the multiplication of special offerings of lambs and bullocks, included taking two leaven loaves of bread and waving them before the Lord at the altar. Use of leaven in the other feasts was upon penalty of excommunication, but here, strangely enough, God is commanding that leaven was to be in these bread offerings. Remember, under the law nothing leavened could be offered with a blood sacrifice at the altar. In our study of Unleavened Bread, we learned that leaven spoke of anything that was hypocritical, evil, false, corrupting and destructive.

Why was leaven commanded at Pentecost? Because Pentecost has to do with the church, whereas Passover had to do with Christ. There was no leaven when anything referred to

Christ because there was no sin in Him. When the Scripture refers to leaven here, it is because of God's recognition (and it should be the believer's recognition) that **the root of sin has not yet been eradicated, even though at Passover the blood was applied and you were cleansed from your sin; at Unleavened Bread the old man was put off and its dominating power in your life was broken; and in Firstfruits you were to begin to implement righteousness in your new life in Christ. AT PENTECOST WE RECOGNIZE THAT THE FALLEN SIN NATURE IS STILL PRESENT, AND THE COMING OF THE HOLY SPIRIT IS TO ARREST THE ACTION OF SIN IN THE BELIEVER'S LIFE. THIS IS WHY JESUS SAID THAT WHEN THE HOLY SPIRIT WOULD COME HE WOULD CONVICT OF SIN, OF RIGHTEOUSNESS AND OF JUDGMENT. THE HOLY SPIRIT COMES TO RETARD SIN IN OUR LIFE AND TO BUILD AND TO IMPLEMENT RIGHTEOUSNESS IN US, TO TEACH US WHAT IT MEANS TO CEASE FROM LIVING BY THE CREATED LIFE WHICH WE HAD BY THE BIRTH OF THE FLESH AND TO LEARN TO LIVE BY THE LIFE OF THE SPIRIT THAT WE HAVE BY THE NEW BIRTH IN JESUS.**

Reckon yourselves to be dead indeed unto sin, but alive unto God through Jesus Christ our Lord.
Rom. 6:11

Know ye not, that to whom ye yield yourselves servants to obey, his servants ye are to whom ye obey; whether of sin unto death, or of obedience unto righteousness? But God be thanked, that you were the servants of sin, but you have obeyed from the heart that form of doctrine which was delivered you. But then made free from sin, you became the servants of righteousness. I speak after the manner of men because of the infirmity of your flesh: for as you have yielded your members servants to uncleanness and to iniquity unto iniquity: even so now yield your members servants to righteousness unto holiness. For when you were the servants of sin, you were free from righteousness. What fruit had ye then in those things whereof you are now ashamed? For the end of those things is death. But now being made free from sin, and become servants to God, you have your fruit unto holiness, and the end everlasting life. Rom. 6:16–22

In other words, the exhortation is that we are to no longer yield to the sin that is still present with us. Wherefore, Romans 8:2 says, **"For the law of the Spirit of life in Christ Jesus has made me free from the law of sin and death."** We are no longer under the dominating power of the fallen nature. We do not have to yield to sin as long as we have the Spirit of Christ within us. There are certain patterns of sin that a non-Christian might exchange for another, but he cannot really overcome sin. The American Medical Association today recognizes that the vast majority of physical health problems of the American population can be attributed to unresolved guilt and the chemical reactions which that causes in the body. *Sin is with us but we don't have to be dominated by it.* Colossians 1:1-13 talks about the power of the gospel and of Christ to set us free from the power of sin by the power of the Holy Spirit.

Leaven at Pentecost teaches us that sin is present. Many Christians who have not been baptized in the Holy Spirit and have wondered about its validity have asked in their heart, "Well, if you really have the Holy Spirit, then why aren't you perfect? Why are there still problems? I look at Pentecostal Christians and see problems in their life, I see character weaknesses, I see things that are not glorifying to God." So what? God already knew about that! This is why leaven is present at the Feast of Pentecost. **THE PENTECOSTAL EXPERIENCE IS A NECESSARY STEP, BUT IT IS NOT WHAT TAKES US BEYOND THE EXPERIENCE OF SIN.** As we continue in this series of studies, it will be seen that NO LEAVEN IS FOUND IN THE FEAST OF TABERNACLES. IT IS UNDER THIS FEAST THAT THE CHURCH IS BROUGHT TO MATURITY AND PERFECTION BY THE ATONING BLOOD OF JESUS, THE WORD OF GOD AND THE MINISTRY OF THE HOLY SPIRIT. It is at the Feast of Tabernacles that the believer comes to completion. This feast has never been kept in the history of the church. It involves the Feast of Trumpets, the Day of Atonement and Tabernacles.

There were two wave loaves. Two in the Scripture is the number of witness, the number of testimony. When Jesus sent out His disciples, they were always sent out two-by-two (Luke 9 and 10). Also, Jesus said that in the mouth of two or three witnesses must every word be established. As we read earlier in Ephesians, the two loaves speak of a formation in the Body of Christ where Jesus, through the Cross, would take Jew and Gentile and make them one as a testimony to the unregenerate world of the power of Christ.

There is a dual witness going forth in the earth and some are not seeing it. Many people have difficulty with prophecy because they don't keep this in mind. There is both a natural covenant and a spiritual covenant with Abraham, and the Church of Jesus Christ is fulfilling that spiritual covenant. The existing nation of Israel is in the process of finding fulfillment of the natural covenant with Abraham, and the natural covenant, in its fulfillment and completion, will bring the spiritual and the natural into one. No one who is intellectually honest can read the prophecies of the Word of God written thousands of years ago and look at the history of Israel in this generation, fulfilling scripture prophecy after prophecy in perfect order, and not recognize divine design and providence. Israel as a restored nation is one witness. The second witness comes from the Church of Jesus Christ making the clarion call of the gospel around the world. This has come in the wake of the Pentecostal Revival beginning at the turn of the century, as the church has accomplished more in missions and evangelism than at any time since the first century.

Not only were there two wave offerings, but there were also two tenth deals of fine flour. Another example of this measure in the Scripture was the two omers of manna gathered on the 6th day that fed the children of Israel in the wilderness. The showbread in the tabernacle of Moses was composed of two tenth deals of flour and speaks of a double portion. It also speaks of the kingly–priestly anointing of the priesthood of Melchezidek, which was Christ's order of priesthood. Also, a double anointing and double portion go with the birthright.

You and I are members of the church of the first–born, which means as Christians we receive a particular anointing, a particular placement and a particular privilege in the household of God. The first–born's privilege was a double portion of the natural inheritance, the kingly ruling authority and the priestly ministering responsibility. We are the church of the first–born; therefore, we will rule and reign with Christ. We will also serve with Him in the tabernacle of God in the heavenlies and receive the double portion as joint heirs with Christ.

Sign and Seal

Pentecost was a sign and a seal. The men had to be circumcised on the eighth day in order to keep the law of Moses. That was the sign of keeping the law of covenant. There is a sign and a seal for keeping the new covenant in Christ: the Baptism in the Holy Spirit with the evidence of speaking in other tongues. The following are some verses that verify this.

In whom [Jesus] you also trusted, after that you heard the word of truth, the gospel of your salvation: in whom also after that you believed, you were sealed with that holy Spirit of promise, which is the earnest of our inheritance until the redemption of the purchased possession, unto the praise of his glory.
Eph. 1:13–14

Now he which stablishes us with you in Christ, and has anointed us, is God; who has also sealed us, and given the earnest of the Spirit in our hearts.
II Cor. 1:21–22

The Baptism of the Holy Spirit is an earnest of the double portion that is to come. I don't know a Christian baptized in the Holy Spirit who says that he has mined the depths of the gift of the Baptism. I know in my experience that I have not mined the depths of that one particular gift from the Lord, and the Scripture says that it is just an earnest of our inheritance.

If you want to buy a parcel of land, the owner wants to know that you have the capacity to perform. Why would he want to tie the land up in a contract with you unless he has reason to believe that you can pay the price in the time frame that is decided upon? One of the things that he will require is an earnest while you prepare to pay the rest of the price.

THE BAPTISM OF THE HOLY SPIRIT IS AN EARNEST OF OUR INHERITANCE TO LET US KNOW THAT ALL THE REST OF THE PROMISES IN THE BOOK ARE GOING TO BE PERFORMED IN THE FULLNESS OF TIME! How do you know you're going to get these promises? What does Christ give you to let you know? Besides the fact that He is a person of integrity who will not violate His word, who has entered a covenant by His blood and laid down His life to make that covenant for you, and placed His life in you so that you could receive of Him and walk in Him, He has given you an assurance that He will do all He said He would do, and **that is the seal of the covenant in the Baptism of the Holy Spirit.**

What does "fine flour" mean in the Scripture? Fine flour originates from the whole wheat kernel. They took the kernel and got rid of the outer crust and straw. There had to be a grinding to break the outer shell; they would then take the wheat and put it in a concrete or rock wheel to crush it and grind it to make a fine flour.

"Bread corn is bruised" (Is. 28:28). I Corinthians 10:17 says that we are all made to be partakers of that one bread. If our life in Christ is to be food for others, how are we as single kernels of wheat to be made into a loaf of bread except our lives be blended? How can our life be something that the lost weary traveler in the world can feed upon? The only way he will have something to feed upon in our life is for the outer shell to be crushed and broken so that the inner meat can be released.

What is the outer shell? The old man, Adam. On the inside, in the innermost being, is where Christ was birthed when you were saved, and through the Baptism of the Holy Spirit something is going to happen: "After that the Holy Spirit is come upon you, you shall receive power and you shall be my witnesses" (Acts 1:8). You shall receive divine enablement to be His martyrs, which means that the outer man is to be perishing while the inner man is renewed day by day. "All my plans, ambitions and wishes at my feet in ashes lay," the hymn writer wrote. **There must be a dying to self so that the life of God, the beauty of Christ, the self–denying love of God, can begin to be released in and through you and you can have fruit to give, or bread to feed the weary traveler.**

A singing contest once took place during which a well-known opera star came out and sang that beautiful hymn, "Amazing Grace." Every note was perfect, he had beautiful voice control, the rise and fall of his volumn was perfect as he expressed the meaning of that music. The audience stood up and applauded him for a few minutes and he sat down. Then this old man came out to sing. He had a crackling voice, he missed a couple of notes here and there, he didn't have the control and training of the opera star; but as he sang, tears streamed down his cheeks and there was a brokenness in his voice which touched the heart chords of that audience. They wept and gave him a standing ovation and brought him back three times. Of course, they gave the prize to this old man with the crackling voice. Afterwards, he and the opera star were talking back stage and the old man said, "You know, I wish I could sing like you do. Your voice is so perfect, every note was right, beautiful voice control, you sang it so well." *The opera star said, "Yes, every note was perfect. I really knew the song, but you knew the songwriter, and that's the difference."* The same song; one fed spiritually and one did not. It would be nice to have all of that perfect talent and to feed spiritually also, but if you have to make a choice, choose the spiritual.

In order to feed, you have to die to self. The end of Hebrews 5 says, "Strong meat belongs to them who by reason of use have exercised their senses to discern both good and evil, but milk belongs to those who are unskillful in the word of righteousness." One day the pig and the chicken were going along the country road and decided to be a real blessing to the old country preacher that day. The chicken looked at the pig and said, "Why don't we go by early this morning and give that preacher a nice breakfast of ham and eggs?" The pig said, "You know, for you that's real commitment, but for me it's total sacrifice." You might say that's the difference between milk and meat. If your life is going to feed, it's going to cost you something. If you're going to go on beyond Pentecost, you will have to hear this message. To give meat, it costs the life of the one who gives it. You have to invest your life. Jesus said, "If any man come after me, let him deny himself, take up his cross and follow me. He that seeks to save his life will lose it, but he that loses his life for my sake and the gospel's shall find it."

The fine flour speaks of the trials, testings, temptations, sufferings, denials and the going the extra mile to feed, but fine flour is not enough. It was to be baked with leaven, the process which intensifies the unity.

> I indeed baptize you with water unto repentance: but he that comes after me is mightier than I, whose shoes I am not worthy to bear: he shall baptize you with the Holy Ghost, and with fire: Whose fan is in his hand, and he will thoroughly purge his floor, and gather his

wheat into the garner; but he will burn up the chaff with unquenchable fire. Matt. 3:11-12

The chaff in your life needs to be burned out. That is not a negative experience; that which is really from the Lord will not be consumed in the fire. We need the Baptism of the Holy Spirit and if we get it as God intends, we get more than tongues. When Jesus received His Baptism in the Holy Spirit, the Spirit remained on Him. He received the Spirit in fullness, without measure, and immediately the Spirit drove Him into the wilderness. After fasting and praying for 40 days, the devil met Him and He was tested in spirit, soul and body and passed the test in every realm. **Before every promotion you have a successful test. Every time God gives you something, know that if you want to possess it and keep it as an abiding part of your life, you will have to pass the coming test that goes with it.**

Jesus passed these tests and the Scripture says in Luke 4 that He returned in the power of the Spirit. People say, "I want the Holy Ghost and power. How do I get the power?" Pass the test; pay the price; go far enough; get past the tongues; get past the blessing. LET THE HOLY SPIRIT BURN OUT THE CHAFF AND DEAL WITH YOUR FLESH AND BRING YOU INTO SUBMISSION TO HIS WILL AND LEARN HOW TO FACE THE TESTS THAT WILL TEMPT YOU TO COME OUT OF THAT SURRENDER. WHEN YOU DO, AND TO THE DEGREE THAT YOU DO, GOD THE HOLY SPIRIT WILL COMMIT HIS POWER INTO YOUR LIFE. Because Jesus did it perfectly, He had perfect power. Power and purity go together. If you have power without purity, you will burn out and won't stand. You must have character. Many people have gotten hold of the power of the Spirit to a degree but have not allowed the fire of the Spirit to work and burn out the wrong motivations, wrong attitudes and self-righteousness.

The Baptism of the Holy Spirit is not just to receive blessings, but it has a purpose spoken of by the fine flour and of being baked in order to bring in purity and union. When you are really filled with the Spirit of God and allow Him to do His work, you will allow Him to blend your life in His body with vital, meaningful spiritual relationships related to divine purpose.

We have talked about this being a firstfruit feast, the promise of a greater fruit to come. It was a wave offering before the Lord, and its parallel was the Baptism of the Holy Spirit where the power of the Spirit comes upon us.

Holy to the Lord

> And the priest shall wave them with the bread of the firstfruits for a wave offering before the Lord, with the two lambs: they shall be holy to the Lord for the priest. Lev. 23:20

Even though these bread loaves contain leaven, the Lord looks upon them as if they are holy. This means that before God, you are accepted in a state of holiness even though sin is at work in your life. How can God do that and be honest? **Because He is going to remove that sin out of your life.**

The First Harvest Period

> And thou shalt keep the feast of weeks unto the Lord thy God with a tribute of a freewill offering of thine hand, which thou shalt give unto the Lord thy God, according as the Lord thy God hath blessed thee. Deut. 16:10

> Also in the day of the firstfruits, when you bring a new meat offering unto the Lord, after your weeks be out [Pentecost], you shall have a holy convocation: ye shall do no servile work. Num. 28:26

This is not the feast day of firstfruits back at Passover but the harvest of those fruits come to maturity. The spring rains bring the winter crops, the firstfruits, to maturity. The rain in the fall begins to bring the summer crops to maturity, or to soften the ground for the planting of the next winter crops. Along those lines there are some very important scriptures.

> For the land, whither thou goest in to possess it, is not as the land of Egypt, from where you came out, where you sowed seed and watered it with your foot, as a garden of herbs: but the land whither you go to possess it, is a land of hills and valleys, and drinks water of the rain of heaven: A land which the Lord thy God cares for: the eyes of the Lord thy God are always upon it, from the beginning of the year even unto the end of the year. And it shall come to pass, if ye shall hearken diligently unto my commandments which I command you this day, to love the Lord your God, and to serve him with all your heart and with all your soul,

that I will give you the rain of your land in his due season, the first rain and the latter rain, that you may gather in your corn, and your wine, and your oil. And I will send grass in your fields for your cattle, that you may eat and be full. Deut. 11:10–15

The Lord shall open unto you his good treasure, the heaven to give the rain unto your land in his season, and to bless all the work of your hand: and you shall lend unto many nations, and you shall not borrow. Deut. 28:12

There is a spiritual significance:

Be glad then, ye children of Zion, and rejoice in the Lord your God: for he has given you the former rain moderately, and he will cause to come down for you the rain, the former rain, and the latter rain in the first month. Joel 2:23

A double portion of the outpouring of the Spirit is to come. This is a prophecy which was quoted by Peter on the Day of Pentecost when he said that this outpouring of the Holy Spirit, this double portion that we are receiving, is a fulfillment, at least in part, of Joel's prophecy. The outpouring of the Holy Spirit, then, is likened unto the rain to bring forth a harvest, to bring it to maturity. God pours out the blessing from His Spirit because He wants to produce fruit in your life: the fruit of character and the fruit of souls.

Come, and let us return unto the Lord: for he has torn, and he will heal us; he has smitten, and he will bind us up. After two days will he revive us: in the third day he will raise us up, and we shall live in his sight. Then shall we know, if we follow on to know the Lord: his going forth is prepared as the morning; and he shall come unto us as the rain, as the latter and former rain unto the earth. Hosea 6:1–3

This speaks of the outpouring of the Holy Spirit; **it speaks of the Lord coming to us spiritually in times and seasons of refreshing and revival,** and it is a spiritual counterpart for Pentecost. When you receive the Baptism of the Holy Spirit, one of the things that immediately begins to follow in your life is a firstfruit harvest. You find changes in your heart; you find a new sensitivity to God and a new love for Him that you hadn't had before; you find a change of motivations and new desires.

People who get baptized in the Holy Spirit and don't study the Word knock on my office door or call me on the phone and say, "I was just worshipping the Lord and something came on me and I began to weep and cry, and I don't know what it was." I know what it was. The Holy Spirit was beginning to teach them what it means to travail and to intercede. They didn't understand that it was the love of God beginning to be released in their spirit, the burden of intercession. I promise you that until you learn to intercede in the Holy Spirit for a lost and dying world, you won't even begin to know the love of God. We think we know God's love when we receive His blessings. However, when God begins to break your heart for a person who you have never known with a love that is so demanding, so constraining and so compelling that you can't take it, then you begin to know a little of God's love. It will cause you to intercede and travail to the point where you say, "God, lift it, I cannot carry it." This is one way the Lord comes to us in the early and latter rain and begins to bring fruit.

> It will come to pass afterward I will pour out my Spirit upon all flesh; and your sons and your daughters shall prophesy, your old men shall dream dreams, your young men shall see visions: and upon the servants and upon the handmaids in those days will I pour out my Spirit. Joel 2:28–29

God will pour out of His Spirit in a great and mighty way, which is part of what has been happening in this present Pentecostal outpouring. It is what happened in the early church and it's what happened in the restoration of the church at the turn of this century.

We see then that these seasons of revival, refreshing and renewal of sensitivity to the reality of God's presence and His love shed abroad in our heart compel us to go on and cause many changes in our life. Why did the Apostle Paul press on? Twice he was shipwrecked and left a day and a night in the ocean; he was beaten, stoned and left for dead. Was he a glutton for punishment? No. It wasn't because of pride, because he wasn't glorified or given any honors for it. He didn't get money for what he did. In fact, half of the time he had to support himself. He tells us in one of his epistles to the Corinthians, "The love of God constrains me." GOD'S LOVE WORKING IN HIM COMPELLED HIM TO GO ON. We have to know what it means to be compelled by the Spirit.

...thou shalt keep the feast of weeks unto the Lord thy God with a tribute of a freewill offering of thine hand, which thou shalt give unto the Lord thy God, according as the Lord thy God has blessed thee.
Deut. 16:10

Before I got saved I was at the bottom of the barrel. Everything that I really wanted in life had fallen apart. I was getting the things I thought I wanted and pursued, but I was finding them to be nothing. All of my natural goals were beginning to be achieved right before me, but I was losing everything that I really wanted deep down inside when I began to find out who I was. Some people have it all and they have something to give up. I had nothing to give up, I only had something to gain when I came to Jesus. I had a miserable childhood; I was so devastated by it that the only reason I got up in the morning and went through the motions was because somehow I had a hope that there was an answer for all of my pain. I didn't know what it was but I was willing to search, and that was the only thing I lived for. I couldn't find genuine love, as much as I searched. When I came to the Lord and found Him reaching for me and found His love for me, He captured something in my heart and I made a commitment and said, Lord, I will go wherever you want me to go and I will do whatever you want me to do and I will try to be whatever you want me to be.

I would read in the Scriptures about crowns that saints would have to lay at His feet, and I wanted to have something with which to bless the Lord. I fell in love with Jesus. I don't care too much about what happens in this life as far as the natural is concerned. We all enjoy nice things, but I can take them or leave them. WHAT I REALLY CARE ABOUT IS WHEN IT'S ALL OVER AND DONE AND I STAND AT THE FEET OF THE LORD, I HAVE SOMETHING THAT WILL BLESS HIM — I WANT TO HAVE SHEAVES TO LAY AT HIS FEET, I WANT TO HAVE PLEASED HIS HEART. I DON'T CARE ABOUT HAVING A CROWN TO WEAR ON MY HEAD, BUT I WOULD LIKE TO HAVE ONE TO CAST AT HIS FEET. I have that compelling desire of the heart and when I stand before the Judgment Seat of Christ, I want to have something to give Him. When I first got saved, I had nothing to give. **I remember weeping in my prayer closet saying, "God, give me something to give to bless you." I didn't know it then, but I have come to**

understand that this is what worship is all about. You never really worship biblically unless you have something to give, which is why you bring the freewill offering with what the Lord has blessed you with. I don't have anything to give in the natural; the only reason I will ever have anything to give is because of what God by His grace has wrought in me. If someone comes to the Lord because of my obedience to the Spirit, it isn't me, it's His grace that worked through me and touched that life and helped that person to know Jesus. But if I obey Him, I get the credit as far as having something to lay at His feet. That is fruit.

On the Day of Pentecost, 3,000 souls were born into the Kingdom; three days later, 5,000 were added. Later came the great Gentile harvest. I want some souls to lay at Jesus' feet, I want to have something to give to Jesus. I want my character and my life to be pleasing to Him — that is what this Pentecostal harvest is all about, **BUT IT'S THE PROMISE OF A MUCH GREATER HARVEST TO COME.**

In the case of Tabernacles, the final harvest came at the end of the year. Several things concerning this are mentioned in the following Scriptures:

> Let both [tares and wheat] grow together until the harvest: and in the time of harvest I will say to the reapers, Gather ye together first the tares, and bind them in bundles to burn them: but gather the wheat into my barn. Matt. 13:30

> The enemy that sowed them [the tares] is the devil; the harvest is the end of the world; and the reapers are the angels. Matt. 13:39

Jesus was speaking prophetically of the end of the age, and there is a harvest of two kinds of fruit to be reaped.

> But when the fruit is brought forth, immediately he puts in the sickle, because the harvest is come.
> Mark 4:30

> Be patient therefore, brethren, unto the coming of the Lord. Behold, the husbandman waits for the precious fruit of the earth, and has long patience for it, until he receives the early and latter rain. James 5:7

This prophesies of the coming of the early and the latter rain. The outpouring of the Spirit comes so rapidly that it will bring the fruit to harvest, and we are now coming to that day.

73

PENTECOST, THEN, IS A POURING OUT OF THE SPIRIT, THE PURPOSE AND INTENT OF WHICH IS TO BRING AN INITIAL HARVEST WITH A PROMISE OF A GREATER HARVEST TO COME. I ask you, do you have any harvest sheaves to present to the Master's feet? He wants you to enter into His Kingdom with an abundance to give.

Pentecost is an outpouring of the rain but if there is no crop that follows, then there is no purpose in the rain! God didn't baptize you in the Holy Spirit so you can talk in tongues and not be changed. THERE IS TO BE A CHANGE IN YOUR CHARACTER AND, BECAUSE OF IT, THERE IS TO BE A CHANGE IN THE EFFECTIVENESS OF YOUR LIFE BECAUSE YOU HAVE BECOME BREAD THAT WILL FEED THE WEARY TRAVELER. YOU HAVE SOMETHING TO GIVE — YOU'RE NOT EMPTY. FREELY YOU HAVE RECEIVED, FREELY GIVE.

Pentecost, then, is a glorious and powerful feast. It allows us to have firstfruits, to taste of them, to produce something, but it is not the end. Leaven is still present, the imperfections are still present, and we must recognize that the fruits which we taste at Pentecost are also prophetic of the greater harvest to come where there is no leaven.

If you haven't come this far in your experiential relationship with the Lord, everything else that is taught in this book will become mere theory for you. It will work as hope, it will feed your faith, and I trust will help you to grow. God's desire is not for you to just have a Pentecostal experience; He wants you to go on and keep the Feast of Tabernacles. **GO ALL THE WAY WITH JESUS, MOVE IN AND LAY HOLD OF THE GREATER HARVEST THAT IS AVAILABLE FOR YOUR LIFE. GO THROUGH THE TESTINGS, THE FASTING AND PRAYER, THE BURNING OUT OF THE DROSS; COME BACK IN THE POWER OF THE SPIRIT WITH FRUITFULNESS FOLLOWING IN YOUR LIFE BOTH IN CHARACTER AND SOULS, AND PREPARE TO GO ON UNTIL THAT DAY WHEN THE FEAST OF TABERNACLES IS KEPT. THE SOUNDING OF TRUMPETS IS THE CALL TO KEEP THE FEAST OF TABERNACLES. THOSE WHO HAVE EARS TO HEAR AND CAN SEE THE SIGNS OF THE TIMES IN LIGHT OF THE WORD WILL KNOW THAT THE TRUMPET HAS ALREADY SOUNDED. IT'S TIME TO PREPARE TO KEEP THE FEAST OF THE DAY OF ATONEMENT.**

Father, so many have come this far and have camped. I pray that you will stir each heart and build in them a vision of faith that will carry them on to the greater harvest promised by Pentecost. Disturb the present to improve the future and awaken each heart to the sound of the trumpet call of the Spirit in this day. Grant unto us the grace and sensitivity to respond and appropriate all that you have intended. Amen.

THE FEAST OF TABERNACLES

As an overview, there were three feast periods. The first one was Passover in the first month on the Jewish calendar, consisting of Passover, Unleavened Bread and Firstfruits. Fifty days later we come to Pentecost in the third month. Following Pentecost was the Feast of Tabernacles beginning on the first day of the seventh month with the Day of Trumpets. On the tenth of the month we have the Day of Atonement, followed by the feast period of Booths, also called Tabernacles.

The first four feasts all related historically to Israel: At Passover they came up out of Egypt, and at Pentecost they met God and came into covenant relationship with Him as a nation at Mt. Sinai.

These feasts had a prophetic significance: Christ was crucified on Passover, buried on Unleavened Bread, rose again on Firstfruits, and the outpouring of the Holy Spirit took place on the Day of Pentecost when the early church was formed.

You and I have also kept those feasts by coming to Calvary, letting the old man be buried and turning away from sin, following after the Lord and walking in newness of life, and receiving the Baptism in the Holy Spirit.

The Feast of Tabernacles had no historical fulfillment for Israel, nor has it had historical fulfillment for the church. THESE LAST THREE FEASTS IN THE SEVENTH MONTH (7 always being the number of completion in God's means of communicating with us) ARE MEANT TO COVER THE EVENTS WHICH DEAL WITH THE SECOND COMING OF CHRIST. There are two areas here that we must understand. People get confused with the end–time events in Tabernacles because they don't understand a basic principle of prophecy.

All of Bible prophecy is an unveiling of covenant obligation that God has with His people. God relates to us by covenants. All of the prophecies that are unveiling today are mostly fulfillments from three covenants: first, the Abrahamic covenant which was reconfirmed and enlarged upon with the Mosaic covenant, which again was enlarged upon and fulfilled with the Davidic covenant, finding their fulfillment in the new covenant in Christ. That which is unfulfilled or still prophetic in the Word of God deals with covenant obligations that God has not yet completed.

Concerning the Abrahamic covenant, God told Abraham that his seed would be as the **stars of the sky and as the sand of the sea,** creating a dual covenant. One was a covenant that would concern *a* seed after the flesh, **which became the nation of Israel through the promised child Isaac. We see fulfillment of that covenant obligation still taking place today with the restoration of Israel in our generation.** Abraham also had a covenant for *a spiritual seed,* wherefore Christ spoke to the Israelites who did not believe, "If you were of your father Abraham, you would do the works of Abraham," showing that they did not have the character or spirit of Abraham. The spiritual seed as **the stars of the sky would have this character of Abraham. This covenant obligation is being fulfilled in the church.** The physical and spiritual were meant to be one but because of the apostacy of Israel, because of their refusal to be a channel to reach a Gentile world and their rejection of the Lord Jesus Christ, God provided a way for the Gentiles through Christ in His church.

In this church age, the ministry emphasis is to the Gentile world. It will come to conclusion at the end of the church age, at which time God will deal with the apostate church and apostate Israel in what is called the Tribulation period. At the end of that Tribulation period, apostate Israel will turn back to God and recognize Christ as their Messiah and He will set up His millennial kingdom. That is prophetic obligation.

Tabernacles, therefore, has a dual area of literal fulfillment that must come. One is directly related to the physical seed of Israel and one is directly related to that spiritual seed, which we are in the church. The Scripture tells us that we are spiritual Israel, we are the circumcision in the Spirit. This dual application has been seen all the way through from Passover to Pentecost.

For the physical seed, Israel, the Day of Trumpets speaks of the regathering of Israel as a nation, which we will focus upon in the next section. The Day of Atonement speaks of Israel's turning to Christ, and the Feast of Booths speaks of the millennial reign. The application of the Feast of Tabernacles to us as a church is a little different, although it has its parallel. There are several emphases for the church at this season, of which we will take note.

1. *The Word*

    And Moses wrote this law, and delivered it unto the

priests the sons of Levi, which bare the ark of the covenant of the Lord, and unto all the elders of Israel. And Moses commanded them, saying, At the end of every seven years, in the solemnity of the year of release, in the feast of tabernacles, when all Israel is come to appear before the Lord thy God in the place which he shall choose, thou shalt read this law before all Israel in their hearing. Deut. 31:9-11

Take this book of the law, and put it in the side of the ark of the covenant of the Lord your God, that it may be there for a witness against thee. Deut. 31:26

Under the law, every seventh year was a sabbath year, a year of rest. There was not to be any work. They wouldn't harvest or plant the fields but would let them rest in the seventh year. In that year, there was to be a special reading of the book of the law, the first five books of the Bible written by Moses, kept in the side of the ark of the covenant in the Holy of Holies. The book of the law was taught every week, but there was a special emphasis in the seventh year at Tabernacles.

When you are come unto the land which the Lord thy God gives thee, and shall possess it, and shall dwell therein, and shall say, I will set a king over me, like as all the nations that are about me; and it shall be, when he sitteth upon the throne of his kingdom, that he shall write him a copy of this law in a book out of that which is before the priests the Levites: And it shall be with him, and he shall read therein all the days of his life: that he may learn to fear the Lord his God, to keep all the words of this law and these statutes, to do them: that his heart be not lifted up above his brethren, and that he turn not aside from the commandment, to the right hand, or to the left: to the end that he may prolong his days in his kingdom, he, and his children, in the midst of Israel.
Deut. 17:14; 18-20

The book of law was also kept in the throne of the king of Israel to be read and studied day and night. This pictures the responsibility of the ministry to teach the Word of God to the people. It is clear that **the Feast of Tabernacles will bring a special emphasis and illumination in the opened Book,**

the Word of God. As we enter into this feast period and keep it as the church, we see that it will be characterized as a time when God will bring special emphasis and illumination upon the Book.

> And beginning at Moses and all the prophets, he expounded unto them in all the scriptures the things concerning himself. Luke 24:27

> And he said unto them, These are the words which I spoke unto you, while I was yet with you, that all things must be fulfilled, which were written in the law of Moses, and in the prophets, and in the psalms, concerning me. Then opened he their understanding, that they might understand the scriptures.
> Luke 24:44–45

One of the things **signified by Tabernacles** which we must recognize is that there is **a special witness of the Word,** a special ministry and teaching in the Word, a special anointing of the Spirit to open up the understanding of the Word; not truth that wasn't written before, but **NEW ILLUMINATION UPON THE TRUTH WILL COME IN ORDER TO BRING THE CHURCH TO COMPLETION AT THE FEAST OF TABERNACLES.** God has a special set time in which He will bring this emphasis and illumination in the Word.

There are times in the history of the church and in the history of God's people in their relationship with Him when there has been no open revelation, no Word from heaven. In our country, that was the condition across the nation, in almost every church, in the 1950's. Even the Pentecostal churches, **because they had not gone on from Pentecost to the greater harvest,** dried up and became as tinkling brass. Young people said, "If this is all there is to it, it's got to be elsewhere," and an entire generation began to fall into other kinds of spiritual endeavors, hungry for spiritual reality and spiritual experience — because the church had not gone on to the Feast of Tabernacles, because there was no open revelation of the Book. There were a few forerunners, a few Calebs and Joshuas, who had eyes to see after the Spirit and could see what was coming, but when they taught it, it wasn't heard or understood because the people weren't ready. I believe we are in a day when that has changed.

One of the major things we recognize, then, is that this is a feast of the open Book. It is a time when understanding of the Scriptures should begin to leap out at us as we study them and as we wait before the Lord.

We also see in I Kings 8 something else that happened which was very special. We study the presence of God and the ark of the covenant in Moses Tabernacle, which was dedicated at Passover. We see it go into David's Tabernacle upon Mt. Zion. The first 11 verses of this chapter tell about the dedication of Solomon's temple.

2. *The Glory of the Lord*

> Then Solomon assembled the elders of Israel, and all the heads of the tribes, the chief of the fathers of the children of Israel, unto king Solomon in Jerusalem, that they might bring up the ark of the covenant of the Lord out of the city of David, which is Zion. And all the elders of Israel came, and the priests took up the ark. And they brought up the ark of the Lord, and the tabernacle of the congregation. And king Solomon, and all the congregation of Israel, that were assembled unto him, were with him before the ark, sacrificing sheep and oxen, that could not be told nor numbered for the multitude. And they drew out the staves, that the ends of the staves were seen out in the holy place before the oracle, and they were not seen without: and there they are unto this day.

Those staves which carried the ark were removed, meaning that the ark would move no more; it came to a resting place.

> It came to pass, when the priests were come out of the holy place, that the cloud filled the house of the Lord. So that the priests could not stand to minister because of the cloud: for the glory of the Lord had filled the house of the Lord. I Kings 8:1–11

As Solomon went to dedicate the temple, the glory of God came and filled the temple in such a way that the priests could not stand to minister. They were slain in the power of the Spirit as the glory of the Lord was revealed — and it took place in the Feast of Tabernacles.

Moses' Tabernacle had been dedicated in the Feast of Passover and dealt with Christ and His atoning work. Solomon's Tabernacle points not only to Christ but it deals more specifically with the church. **It points to a final dedication of the church when Jesus, as the ark of God,** will take His place in the church – **THE FULLNESS OF CHRIST IN HIS PEOPLE** – and that is the time when the church will experience the fullness of the glory of the Lord. Paul talks about how he travails until Christ be fully formed in us; **there is a fullness, a completion to come.**

3. *Spiritual Vision, Unity, Fear of the Lord, and Harvest*

> Arise, shine; for thy light is come, and the glory of the Lord is risen upon thee. For, behold, the darkness shall cover the earth, and gross darkness the people: but the Lord shall arise upon thee, and his glory shall be seen upon thee. And the Gentiles shall come to thy light, and kings to the brightness of thy rising. Lift up thine eyes round about, and see: all they gather themselves together, they come to thee: thy sons shall come from far, and thy daughters shall be nursed at thy side. Then thou shalt see, and flow together, and thine heart shall fear, and be enlarged; because the abundance of the sea shall be converted unto thee, the forces of the Gentiles shall come unto thee.

Then thou shalt see: *SPIRITUAL VISION.* And flow together: *UNITY.* Thine heart shall fear: *THE FEAR OF THE LORD* is the beginning of wisdom, departure from evil is the understanding thereof. The abundance of the sea: *THE MASSES OF HUMANITY HARVESTED.* This is a prophecy of one of the greatest harvests of souls that the world will ever know. Did Jesus speak of this?

> That they all may be one; as thou, Father, art in me, and I in thee, that they also may be one in us: that the world may believe that you have sent me. And the glory which you gave me I have given them; that they may be one, even as we are one: I in them, and you in me, that they may be made perfect in one; and that the world may know that thou hast sent me, and hast loved them, as thou hast loved me. Father, I will that they also, whom thou hast given me, be with me where I am; that they may behold my glory, which thou hast given me: for thou lovedst me before the foundation of the world. John 17:21–24

There is the glory of the Lord to come, a pure vision, a completion, a fullness, a unity, and a great witness to the world. Jesus prayed for this. Its fulfillment is pre–Rapture, because the unity spoken of in John 17 and prophesied by Isaiah will have no effect on a lost world if the people spoken of are not here but in heaven.

4. *Victory Over Sin, Restoration, Keeping the Feasts*

> Husbands, love your wives, even as Christ also loved the church, and gave himself for it; that he might sanctify and cleanse it with the washing of water by the word, that he might present it to himself a glorious church, not having spot, or wrinkle, or any such thing; but that it should be holy and without blemish.
> Eph. 5:25–27

There is victory over sin. In order to see this more clearly, let us look at another significant time in these feast periods, the restoration of Israel. There are four restoration books in the Old Testament: Ezra, Nehemiah (the historical books of restoration), Haggai and Zechariah (the two prophets of the restoration). In Jewish history, there was a time when the Jews would return from Babylonian captivity and the city of Jerusalem would be restored. At the dedication of Solomon's Temple, the glory of the Lord entered the temple at the Feast of Tabernacles, 120 trumpeters blew their horns and were all in one accord. There is a parallel in the dedication of the beginning church with 120 in the upper room, where the speaking of tongues was likened unto a trumpet and the glory of the Lord filled the new covenant temple.

However, during Israel's history Solomon's Temple became defiled by sin and idolatry. The people fell away from God and His patterns and standards of love and righteousness, and the glory of the Lord eventually departed (Ezekiel 8–11). The temple was there, the ritual was there, the people were there, but they were in idolatry and sin and God was not with them. So it is in church history. Once the glory departed Solomon's Temple, it came under judgment and was destroyed when King Nebuchanezzer of Babylon came in and took Israel captive for 70 years.

The church also went into a place of backsliding, into the Dark Ages, and was bound in darkness. In time, Israel's captivity ended and God sent a messenger to call His people out of Babylon to the City of God. It was a message of restoration and began with Ezra. Ezra called, "Let's go back," and a small remnant responded and went back to Jerusalem to rebuild it. **Parallel: There has been a call for God's**

people to come out of Babylon. In the Scripture, Babylon literally means "religious confusion." In fact, the Psalms of Ascent deal with "steps out of Babylon." They are the Psalms that were sung as they came out of Babylon and deal with progressive truth coming out of religious confusion. It was a call to restoration to what they once had with God and to go beyond it.

The remnant returned to Jerusalem and began the work of restoration. They first built the altar, then the foundations of the temple and the city and its walls. *There was much opposition that came against them,* but in time their work was completed. Once again, there is a parallel in church history. The Reformation began and people like Martin Luther stood up and said, No, we aren't saved by crawling up some steps and kissing a piece of wood that was supposed to be from Calvary. We are saved by faith in the atoning work of Christ as a foundation of the temple. Following that came the Anabaptists with the truth of water baptism, followed by the Revivalists with the truth of holiness and the Pentecostal Revival at the turn of the century — a restoration pattern leading towards Tabernacles.

All along the way there has been opposition. D.L. Moody used to preach and his wife would stand up and say, "I've seen you drunk!" She would do that to try and destroy his meetings. When the Pentecostal Revival began at the turn of this century, rocks were thrown through windows of churches and children were beaten by neighborhood bullies. As the healing revival began, there was opposition again with all kinds of imitations.

Vitally connected with the restoration of the temple was the keeping of the feasts of the Lord, in particular the Feast of Tabernacles (Ezra 3, Nehemiah 8). One of the main points in these chapters is that all of those who returned from Babylon gathered as one, and it speaks of unity.

> And when the seventh month was come, and the children of Israel were in the cities, the people gathered themselves together as one man to Jerusalem. Ezra 3:1

> So the priests, and the Levites, and the porters, and the singers, and some of the people, and the Neghinims, and all Israel, dwelt in their cities; and when the seventh month came, the children of Israel

were in their cities. And all the people gathered themselves together as one man into the street that was before the water gate; and they spoke unto Ezra the scribe to bring the book of the law of Moses, which the Lord had commanded to Israel. Neh. 7:73–8:1

In Israel they dipped water in the ritual carried out to keep the Feast of Tabernacles. It speaks of what we read in Ephesians 5, the washing of water by the Word. Jesus gave Himself for the church that He might present it to Himself a glorious church without spot, wrinkle or blemish. **We find once again the emphasis of the open Book, the Word applied to bring holiness and victory over sin, and righteousness and integrity in the believer's life.** As one studies these chapters, he will see that they first established an altar of sacrifice, the foundation of blood atonement. Ezra opened the book from the first day of the seventh month, which was the Day of Trumpets. As they studied the Word, they discovered that they were to keep the feasts. In the church, **the Feast of Trumpets brings an opening of the Word and a great understanding to the people of God (also calling us to keep the feasts).**

And on the second day *were gathered together the chief of the fathers of all the people, the priests, the Levites unto Ezra the scribe, even to understand the words of the Law.* And they found written in the law which the Lord had commanded by Moses, that the children of Israel should dwell in booths in the feast of the seventh month: And that they should publish and proclaim in all their cities, and in Jerusalem, saying, Go forth unto the mount, and fetch olive branches, and pine branches, and myrtle branches, and palm branches, and branches of thick trees, to make booths, as it is written. So the people went forth, and brought them, and made themselves booths, every one upon the roof of his house, and in their courts, and in the courts of the house of God, and in the street of the water gate, and in the street of the gate of Ephraim. And all the congregation of them that were come again out of the captivity made booths, and sat under the booths: for since the days of Joshua the son of Nun unto that day had not the children of Israel done so.

And there was very great gladness. Also day by day, from the first day unto the last day, he read in the book of the law of God. And they kept the feast seven days; and on the eighth day was a solemn assembly, according unto the manner. Neh. 8:13–18

They saw from reading the Word that they were neglecting some things, so they changed what they were doing to conform to the Word. If the way you pray, the way you worship, the way you relate to God, the way you relate to your fellow man, does not conform to the Word of God, you need to adjust. We're in the time period when **we need to get back into the pattern of the Book.**

The church, in coming from Babylonian captivity, must enter in and keep the feasts of the Lord. This is what we have seen in the Reformation up until this day: a systematic pattern of restoration of truth in the perfect order of the feasts as seen in the Word of God.

The foundation of the Lord's house in this period of time was not completed, according to Ezra 3:6–7:

From the first day of the seventh month began they to offer burnt offerings unto the Lord. But the foundation of the temple of the Lord was not yet laid. They gave money also unto the masons, and to the carpenters; and meat, and drink, and oil, unto them of Zidon ...

And when the builders laid the foundation of the temple of the Lord, they set the priests in their apparel with trumpets, and the Levites the sons of Asaph with cymbals, to praise the Lord, after the ordinance of David king of Israel. And they sang together by course in praising and giving thanks unto the Lord; because he is good, for his mercy endures forever toward Israel. And all the people shouted with a great shout, when they praised the Lord, because the foundation of the house of the Lord was laid. Ezra 3:10–11

They didn't shout for nothing. They shouted because they knew the significance of what was happening! We get all excited and jump up and down at the Super Bowl, but somebody gets a little excited in church when something significant takes place and we say they're fanatics. I like what one brother said: More takes place here in one service than in a thousand sessions of the United Nations.

But many of the priests and Levites and chief of the fathers, who were ancient men, that had seen the first house, when the foundation of this house was laid before their eyes, wept with a loud voice; and many shouted aloud for joy: So that the people could not discern that noise of the shout of joy from the noise of the weeping of the people: for the people shouted with a loud shout, and the noise was heard afar off. (vs. 12–13)

They're my type of people! They got excited about something that was significant. The oldtimers were weeping to see it come; the newtimers were glad to see it for the first time in their life and they were shouting with joy. There is a parallel, because the church is progressing into these things in this hour.

This is the historical background. Let's go on and see this overview of the same events from the prophet's viewpoint.

There was opposition as Ezra and Nehemiah came and tried to rebuild the temple and the walls of Jerusalem. As opposition came, the construction of the temple stopped for several years. Instead of building the temple, the people who had returned to Jerusalem decided it was time to build their own houses, with the result that God withheld the early and the latter rains and no grain came in from the crops.

Thus speaketh the Lord of hosts, saying, This people say, The time is not come, the time that the Lord's house should be built ... Is it time for you, O ye, to dwell in your ceiled houses, and this house lie waste? Now therefore thus saith the Lord of hosts; Consider your ways. You have sown much, and bring in little; you eat, but you have not enough; you drink, but you are not filled with drink; you clothe you, but there is none warm; and he that earns wages earns wages to put it into a bag with holes. Thus saith the Lord of hosts; Consider your ways. Go up to the mountain, and bring wood, and build the house; and I will take pleasure in it, and I will be glorified, saith the Lord. Ye looked for much, and lo, it came to little; and when you brought it home, I did blow upon it. Why? saith the Lord of hosts. Because of mine house that is waste, and ye run every man unto his own house. Therefore the heaven over you is stayed from dew, and the earth is stayed from her fruit. Haggai 1:2–10

"Haggai" literally means "feast" or "born of the feast period." As Haggai ministered, the people responded to the Word of the Lord and began to build the Lord's house. This took place in the sixth month. In the seventh month, he again prophesied:

> For thus saith the Lord of hosts; Yet once, it is a little while, and I will shake the heavens, and the earth, and the sea, and the dry land; And I will shake all nations, and the desire of all nations shall come: and I will fill this house with glory, saith the Lord of hosts. The silver is mine, and the gold is mine, saith the Lord of hosts. The glory of this latter house shall be greater than of the former, saith the Lord of hosts: and in this place will I give peace, saith the Lord of hosts.
> Hagg. 2:6–9

The glory of the Lord will fill the restored house, and the glory of the Lord in the house of restoration will be greater than the glory of the former house, Solomon's Temple. There the priests couldn't stand to minister! The power and the glory of God was so great they were all slain. They began to lift up their hands to worship God and His power hit them and they were prostrate before Him. AND THE GLORY OF THE LATTER HOUSE WILL BE GREATER THAN THE FORMER!

Now, the glory of the Spirit of God was manifested in a marvelous and demonstrative way in the early church when it was born, but I want you to know that we're not going out with the kind of glory with which we came in. *We're going out with more than the early church had in its birth.* The church isn't going out the back door with its tail between its legs, backslidden and barely able to survive the pressures of the end of the age. **THE CHURCH OF JESUS CHRIST IS GOING OUT IN VICTORY OVER SIN, VICTORY OVER THIS WORLD AND VICTORY OVER THE DEVIL, CLOTHED IN THE MAJESTY OF JESUS CHRIST, CLOTHED IN HIS POWER AND CLOTHED IN HIS GLORY, DEMONSTRATING HIS CHARACTER TO A LOST AND DYING WORLD WITH THE UNITY JESUS PRAYED FOR IN JOHN 17, THAT THE WORLD MIGHT KNOW THAT GOD HAS LOVED US AS HE DID HIM. WE WILL SEE THE MASSES OF THE SEA CONVERTED IN THE GREATEST HARVEST THE WORLD HAS EVER KNOWN WHEN WE COME INTO THE FULLNESS OF THE FEAST OF TABERNACLES!**

If you begin to understand the significance of this, you'll understand why Israel shouted at the dedication of the restored temple, and you will see that we are the most privileged people who ever walked the face of the earth, for we have the opportunity to see the glory of God in its fullness!

The first verse of the second chapter of Haggai states, "In the seventh month, in the one and twentieth day of the month, came the word of the Lord by the prophet Haggai." This is the last day of the Feast of Tabernacles. We see Jesus' application of the meaning of this in John 7, when on the last day of the Feast He prophesied and said, "If any man thirst, let him come unto me and I will give him water and he will drink, and out of his belly shall flow rivers of living water." It was already foreshadowed in Haggai.

All of this is a parallel of the church in restoration. God's people are not to be concerned about building their own houses or organizations or church groups. They are to be building *God's house:* the family of God, the Body of Christ — not just to grow numerically but to grow spiritually. Unfortunately, many churches are merely spiritual nurseries. People get saved, have their fire insurance and drink the milk of the Word the rest of their lives. They sit in the pew and keep it warm, but they don't want to go on and be all that God wants them to be. God had something to say about this through the prophet Zechariah:

> And it shall come to pass, that every one that is left of all the nations which came against Jerusalem shall even go up from year to year to worship the King, the Lord of hosts, and to keep the feast of tabernacles. And it shall be, that whoso will not come up of all the families of the earth unto Jerusalem to worship the King, the Lord of hosts, even upon them shall be no rain. And if the family of Egypt go not up, and come not, that have no rain; there shall be the plague, wherewith the Lord will smite the heathen that come not up to keep the feast of tabernacles. This shall be the punishment of Egypt, and the punishment of all nations that come not up to keep the feast of tabernacles. In that day shall there be upon the bells of the horses, HOLINESS UNTO THE LORD: and the pots in the Lord's house shall be like the bowls before the altar. Yea, every pot in Jerusalem and in Judah

shall be holiness unto the Lord of hosts: and all they that sacrifice shall come and take of them, and seethe therein: and in that day there shall be no more the Canaanite in the house of the Lord of hosts.

Zech. 14:16–21

This passage is one of the most difficult to interpret in terms of content and time element. The proper laws of interpretation must be heeded. For natural Israel under the old covenant, this prophecy of Zechariah has already been fulfilled, but its picture and principles are to apply to the future. Prophetically, there is sometimes an early fulfillment that gives greater illustration of the more complete fulfillment later on. The promised seed of Abraham was Isaac; the greater seed was Christ.

For natural Israel under the old covenant there was literal fulfillment: a literal temple was built, a literal priesthood was established and literal sacrifices were offered at the restored temple in Jerusalem, and the nations that did not come up came under these judgments. There is an application also to the millennial reign of Christ in Israel. There is also an application for the church, the world–wide body of Christ. The Scripture speaks of the church coming unto the New Jerusalem; we are the church of the firstborn.

From that point of view, we learn that those who do not come up and keep this feast in the seventh month will come under the judgment of the Tribulation period. God ALWAYS gives a way out before judgment comes. You can't see any time when God judged a people without an opportunity for them to first come under his blessings. They reject it and then the judgment comes.

All nations were called annually to go to Jerusalem to worship the Lord. The parallel with the church is that believers from every kindred, every tribe, every nation, every race and every language are to worship the Lord in Spirit and in truth.

> But the hour comes, and now is, when the true worshippers shall worship the Father in spirit and in truth: for the Father seeks such to worship him. God is a Spirit: and they that worship him must worship him in spirit and in truth. John 4:20–24.

Jesus was answering the woman's question, "Should we go to this mountain or do we have to go to Jerusalem to worship?" He was saying it's not in natural Jerusalem but that we are to come to God in spirit and in truth.

> But you are come unto mount Zion, unto the city of the living God, the heavenly Jerusalem, and to an innumerable company of angels, to the general assembly and church of the firstborn, which are written in heaven, and to God the Judge of all, and to the spirits of just men made perfect, and to Jesus the mediator of the new covenant, and to the blood of sprinkling, that speaks better things than that of Abel. Heb. 12:22–24

We are to come into a place of worship and communion with God that was symbolized in that day by the feasts under the heading of Tabernacles. All nations were to keep the Feast of Tabernacles, and to do so they were to follow the order. For us to keep the Feast of Tabernacles we must follow this order. Please hear me: If you are not baptized in the Holy Spirit with the evidence of speaking in other tongues, you will not be able to really keep this feast. It's that important. You cannot keep the Feast of Pentecost unless you have kept the Feast of Passover. No one gets baptized in the Holy Spirit and speaks in other tongues unless they first keep Passover and come under the Blood of the Lamb. You must keep Passover and Pentecost before you can keep Tabernacles.

God wants you to come on in Him. Right now it's easy. You're a new convert, you go right through Passover, Unleavened Bread, Firstfruits, Pentecost, all in one night, but it hasn't always been that way. My mother–in–law, over 70 years of age now, was baptized in the Holy Spirit when she was 12 years old. She remembers several weeks when she prayed late into the night before she received the Baptism. That's the way it was in those days because the season wasn't as it is now and the understanding of those truths wasn't as it is now. So it is that as we go on to keep these truths, the day will come when Trumpets will be easy for anyone, but to come in right now will take some pressing. It will separate the sheep from the goats, and God wants you to come on.

I say this because I want you to hear it in your spirit. To come on means that you have to allow the Holy Spirit to take the Word and apply it to your life. When you see, as did Ezra and Nehemiah, that your life does not conform to certain truths in the Word of God, what will you do? They saw they weren't keeping the feasts and said, "OK, let's go on and keep the feasts," and they started to do it. **We have to become conscientious doers of the Word.** It's not always comfortable because sometimes we have to look at things in our lives that we don't like to face; we want to sweep them under the rug and leave them there, but God comes along and pulls the rug back and says, "Hey, what about this?" We have to become willing to embrace that kind of move and application of the Word and the Spirit of God in our life if we're going to keep Tabernacles.

If the nations failed to keep Tabernacles, the rains of blessing were withheld.

> Ask ye of the Lord rain in the time of the latter rain; so the Lord shall make bright clouds, and give them showers of rain, to every one grass in the field.
> Zech. 10:1

> Come, and let us return unto the Lord: for he has torn, and he will heal us; he has smitten, and he will bind us up. After two days will he revive us: in the third day he will raise us up, and we shall live in his sight. Then shall we know, if we follow on to know the Lord: his going forth is prepared as the morning; and he shall come unto us as the rain, as the latter and former rain unto the earth. Hos. 6:1-3

> Be patient therefore, brethren, unto the coming of the Lord. Behold, the husbandman waits for the precious fruit of the earth, and has long patience for it, until he receive the early and latter rain. James 5:7

The early and latter rain is the outpouring of the Spirit that waters the ground so the fruit matures and ripens. Fruit for the Christian is the fruit of the Spirit — love, joy, peace, longsuffering, gentleness, meekness, tenderness, temperance, faith — or the fruit of souls brought into the Kingdom. **The outpourings of the Spirit, then, are meant to bring about an effectiveness in reaping souls for the Kingdom and for the development of Christian character in our life.**

Those who do not go on to keep the Feast of Tabernacles will find the rain withheld in their lives and a lack of fruit bearing as a result. Refusal to keep the feast at this point, then, brings further judgment. Plagues would come upon them. However, the promise of God to the believer is:

He that dwells in the secret place of the most High shall abide under the shadow of the Almighty. I will say of the Lord, he is my refuge and my fortress: my God; in him will I trust. Surely he shall deliver thee from the snare of the fowler, and from the noisome pestilence. He shall cover thee with his feathers, and under his wings shalt thou trust: his truth shall be thy shield and buckler. Thou shalt not be afraid for the terror by night; nor for the arrow that flies by day; nor for the pestilence that walks in darkness; nor for the destruction that wastes at noonday. A thousand shall fall at thy side, and ten thousand at thy right hand; but it shall not come nigh thee. Only with thine eyes shall you behold and see the reward of the wicked. Because thou hast made the Lord, which is my refuge, even the most High, thy habitation; there shall no evil befall thee, neither shall any plague come nigh thy dwelling. Psalm 91:1 –10

When God says it's time to move on, He shakes things up. When He wanted to get Israel out of Egypt with the promise of blessing and relationship, He sent a few plagues and said, "If you don't let them go, then this is what is going to happen to you." That is why we need a little fear of the Lord. Either we receive deliverance from the domination of a self–centered sinful nature and the redemption that God purchased for us through the death of His Son, or we pay the consequences of rejecting such grace.

It says in the Zechariah prophecy that the pots and bells in the temple were holiness to the Lord. We have to clean up our lives, for we are the temple of God. The Scripture says there are vessels, some of honor and some of dishonor; some of wood and clay; some of silver and brass and gold. The literal translation of this in the Scripture is that some vessels are for special use and some are for common use, like your everyday china and your fine china. These are the kinds of things in the house of God, but all of the pots in God's house will be holiness unto the Lord, which comes because of the Day of Atonement.

The Day of Atonement is very significant here. At Passover, righteousness is imputed unto us and God looks upon us as if we were righteous. You say, "how can He look at me as if I'm righteous? I know I'm not living the life like I should." He does that because you were placed in Christ and under the blood covering. He sees you in Christ, but He doesn't leave you there. You go on to Unleavened Bread, where the old man is crucified; then Firstfruits, where you rise in newness of life; the Baptism of the Holy Spirit, where you are empowered and have a progressive sanctification; and you hear the call of Trumpets to go on to the Day of Atonement, where righteousness is implemented. Booths is the result of that job being finished; it is when the glory comes into the temple with some of the greatest things we will ever see. This has been an overview of the significance of this period in Tabernacles. The next section will show from the Word of God that the Day of Trumpets sounded. Ten days after the Day of Trumpets sounded came the Day of Atonement. The church is somewhere in between right now. Israel regathered as a nation is part of the meaning of Trumpets. Jesus put His capstone on the meaning with another sign, saying that Jerusalem would be trodden down of the Gentiles until the time of the Gentiles be fulfilled. This prophecy alongside the Day of Trumpets has been fulfilled before our very eyes.

This is it — we're headed home and what we're going to do for the Lord, we had better do quickly.

Father, open your Word to our understanding and prepare us for the manifestation of your glory. Draw us together in the unity of the Spirit and the fear of the Lord so that we may receive the harvest that you have intended for our lives. We want to see righteousness fully implemented in our lives and go on to keep this final feast season with all that it implies. Pour out of your grace upon us to will and to do of your good pleasure that you might be fulfilled in us. Amen.

THE FEAST OF TRUMPETS

For Israel, the keeping of this feast was their being regathered as a nation. This is one of the great miracles of the century and is a full story in itself. For our purposes, we will focus on the application of Trumpets for the church.

Before we continue in this section, we must see some things in the Word regarding time elements. We need to see that the Feast of the Day of Trumpets is being kept by the church of Jesus Christ and the prophetic fulfillment of this feast as applied to the church is being fulfilled for the first time in history.

The prophetic application of the Feast of the Day of Trumpets for Israel is their regathering as a nation. This has been occurring since shortly after World War II, when in 1948 Israel became a nation under the U.N. charter. It was in August of 1980 that Jerusalem was finally under the full official rule of Israel, fulfilling the prophecy of Jesus that said Jerusalem would be trodden down of the Gentiles until the times of the Gentiles be fulfilled.

During the Yom Kippur War in 1973 (Yom Kippur is the Day of Atonement on the Israeli calendar) there was a Soviet-backed attack of Syria and Egypt against Israel. It was only a dress rehearsal for the fulfillment of Gog and Magog in Ezekiel. However, some of the wrong elements were present: Iran was pro-Israel and in the United States camp at the time. We have since seen a change. We have also seen a change of government in Ethiopia that was pro-Israel and is now anti-Israel. Egypt is not to be one of the major countries coming against Israel, but they were then. (The present political alignment of these nations now fits that of Ezekiel's prophecy.) There was a Soviet nuclear warship in Cairo Harbor with its warheads pointed towards Israel during this war. When President Nixon called the United States to Red Alert 3, it was enough to cause the Soviet ship to back out of the Cairo Harbor into the Mediterranean Sea.

At the time that this war was about to take place, the cover of Time Magazine reported how an Orthodox Jewish priest was taken by helicopter to Mt. Sinai where he blew the trumpet to announce the seventh month and the coming feast periods. The blowing of the Day of Trumpets was to announce the coming of the Feast of the Day of Atonement ten days later. Being placed on the cover of this world–wide publication was to bring attention to this important time element for the Feast of Trumpets.

Parallel events were taking place in the church in the United States. The Charismatic Renewal was in full motion by then, and I believe that if we understood the Charismatic Renewal we would find its meaning in the Feast of Trumpets.

God has time elements. There are seasons in which He accomplishes things in the earth according to His prophetic program and His divine purposes. This may be illustrated in Hebrews 11, which refers to some who did not receive deliverance in the time of testing.

> And these all, having obtained a good report through faith, received not the promise; God having provided some better thing for us, that they without us should not be made perfect. Heb. 11:39–40

What a tremendous statement that is! God's Word says that there were those who had faith in Him and who had certain things they believed for which God did not allow them to receive; if they received them at that point in their walk with Him, they would have been perfected. God would not allow that to happen in their experience until **we at the end of the age would also be ready to come along. That means that we at the end of the age have some thing better for us because we can experientially enter into this fullness.** There is a time element when God says this can come to pass.

Galatians 4:4 shows this principle with the incarnation of Jesus Christ. In Chapter 3 you read about how Abraham believed in the whole gospel message, having received Isaac back as from the dead, but he didn't receive a new–birth experience because Christ had not yet been born.

> But when the fullness of the time was come, God sent forth his Son, made of a woman, made under the law. Gal. 4:4

> That in the dispensation of the fullness of times he might gather together in one all things in Christ, both which are in heaven, and which are on earth; even in him. Eph. 1:10

There is a time element, which is the first thing we must recognize in the previous feasts which we have looked at as they were fulfilled in history. **We are now looking at**

prophetic feasts which govern the Second Coming of Christ, the first of which has been in the process of fulfillment in this generation.

I want to show you some of the meaning of Trumpets before we begin to look at the feast itself.

> Then whosoever heareth the sound of the trumpet, and taketh not warning; if the sword come, and take him away, his blood shall be upon his own head. He heard the sound of the trumpet, and took not warning; his blood shall be upon him. But he that taketh warning shall deliver his soul. But if the watchman see the sword come, and blow not the trumpet, and the people be not warned; if the sword come, and take any person from among them, he is taken away in his iniquity; but his blood will I require at the watchman's hand. So thou, O son of man, I have set thee a watchman unto the house of Israel; therefore thou shalt hear the word at my mouth, and warn them from me. Ezek. 33:4–7

This shows that the voice of the prophet was likened unto the sound of the trumpet.

> I was in the Spirit on the Lord's day, and heard behind me a great voice, as of a trumpet. Rev. 1:10

This is when the resurrected Christ was speaking to John the truths of the Book of Revelation. The prophetic voice was as the sound of a trumpet.

I Corinthians discusses the gifts of the Spirit and prophecy:

> For if the trumpet give an uncertain sound, who shall prepare himself to the battle? So likewise ye, except ye utter by the tongue words easy to be understood, how shall it be known what is spoken? for ye shall speak into the air. I Cor. 14:8–9

In other words, there should be a strong, clear prophetic utterance.

The time element comes and we have the blowing of the trumpet, **which is a prophetic voice announcing that something is at hand.** We must listen to the warning, and we must hear it. We must recognize that *the beginning of this feast period called Tabernacles is, in God's prophetic timetable, the consummation of His glorious purposes within His people as far as the Church Age is concerned.*

Pentecost was the harvest of firstfruits in the third month preceding Tabernacles. **The feast of the seventh month is the real ingathering of God's great harvest field,** firstfruits being in June and the seventh month being about October when the fruits are gathered. It is a greater harvest than the winter harvest, which comes to fruition in June. The greatest harvest of souls will be at the end of the age, which is almost in itself prophetic of world population increase.

In Numbers 10 we have the institution of the trumpets ministry and see the different functions of it:

> And the Lord spoke to Moses, saying, Make thee two trumpets of silver; of a whole piece shalt thou make them: that thou mayest use them for the calling of the assembly, and for the journeying of the camps. And when they shall blow with them, all the assembly shall assemble themselves to thee at the door of the tabernacle of the congregation. Num. 10:1-3

The number 2 is something that most Bible students have come to understand as the number of witness. It is also the number used throughout the Scripture to speak of Christ in union with His people. The number 4 is the number of creation, 6 is the number of man, 7 is the number of perfection, 3 is the number of the Trinity. Throughout the Scripture these numerics are amazingly consistent. Silver is a metal that is always used to symbolize redemption. There is this dual witness of redemption, symbolized by the two trumpets, which speaks of the period of time when the Day of Trumpets is sounded to announce that **WE ARE COMING INTO THE FEAST OF TABERNACLES, WHEN THE FULLNESS OF GOD'S REDEMPTIVE STORY IS TO BE MANIFEST AND PROCLAIMED THROUGH HIS PEOPLE BY THE POWER OF THE HOLY SPIRIT.**

There are many aspects of this ministry, four of which will be focussed on now.

> And if they blow but with one trumpet, then the princes, which are the heads of the thousands of Israel, shall gather themselves unto thee. Num. 10:4

Calling of the Assembly

Part of verse 2 of this chapter says they would blow the trumpets in order to call the assembly whenever something important had to be shared with the nation. If they were to just call the leaders out of each tribe, they would blow one trumpet and there would be a convocation of leadership. At other times there would be a convocation of the entire assembly and they would come together in the front of the tabernacle area to hear the message. The significance here has to be pictured. Israel had the tabernacle, where God's presence was, in the middle of the camp and the 12 tribes were spread out with three tribes on each side. Whenever the trumpets sounded to call the assembly, the Israelis came out of their tribes and gathered together as one to hear what God was to say. It is prophetic and is picturesque of something.

The Scripture speaks of the Baptism of the Holy Spirit, and in many ways the Pentecostal experience, as a trumpet sound. Something unique has happened in the Charismatic Renewal for the first time in church history. Every great revival has been traced back to one or more leaders: Martin Luther for the Reformation, Wesley, Moody and Finney in different phases of the Restoration. However, beginning in the late 1960's, at the time that Jerusalem became captive of Israel in the Six Day War, the Charismatic Renewal took place without singular leadership. It was a sovereign move of God.

Another unique fact was that the wind of the Spirit blew through every denomination. Many different Christians, no matter which denomination they were in, began to be affected by it. The Charismatic Renewal went over all barriers to break down the walls of denominationalism. It was as if these believers were being called out of their tribes — Catholic, Episcopal, Methodist, Lutheran, Baptist, etc. — and beginning to find their unity in the Body of Christ. That is what the trumpet sound pictured for the church in the calling of the assembly. Its prophetic significance for Israel as a nation, the covenant after the flesh, would be the regathering of Israel as a nation, which also has been taking place during this season.

There is a message in the calling of the assembly. We must recognize that the calling has to be related to the purpose of this hour. The trumpet was sounded to announce the Day of Atonement which was ten days later, the most holy time in Israel's history. We need to understand the message of this call. *It is a call to sanctification and to holy living.* The Charismatic Renewal began without people understanding the call to holiness; they were being called out of their tribes and were gathering together, but they didn't yet know what the message was. Now the message is sounding loud and clear to those who have ears to hear — **it is a call to holiness.**

How does that call to holiness work? I want you to fasten your seat belts because this one will shake you. This cry leaves no one untouched. God is wanting to bring the church on into an experience of sanctification that it has never known in its history. It will not be going back to try to attain what the church was in its beginning. The church is going out with much greater glory, power and understanding than that with which it was born. Part of what we see was prophesied by Isaiah.

> Cry aloud, spare not, lift up thy voice like a trumpet, and show my people their transgression, and the house of Jacob their sins. Yet they seek me daily, and delight to know my ways, as a nation that did righteousness, and forsook not the ordinance of their God: they ask of me the ordinances of justice; they take delight in approaching to God. Isa. 58:1-2

This sounds like a good church! They pray daily, they love the things of the Lord, they want to know His ways, they want justice, they are righteous in that they do righteousness, they don't forsake God's ordinances, and yet the word of the prophet is, "Cry aloud, spare not, lift up thy voice like a trumpet, and show my people their transgression!" There are places in our life that are not pleasing to God. In spite of all of these positive things being described, **it is time to face up to things that are not yet in the likeness and image of Christ.** The first thing that we understand about the meaning of this trumpet sound, which we see by the regathering of Israel as a nation, by the Six Day War, by Israel's taking full possession of Jerusalem and by the Charismatic Renewal on the prophetic timetable, is that the church is being called to a time of extreme sanctification.

The Book of Joshua records how Israel was about to enter the Promised Land to possess the fullness of their inheritance. As they were about to go in, Joshua spoke to them the day before they crossed Jordan:

> And Joshua said unto the people, *Sanctify yourselves for tomorrow the Lord will do wonders among you.* Josh. 3:5

They were going to cross over Jordan on dry ground, and when they got across to the other side they would drive out the enemy.

> And Joshua said, Hereby ye shall know that the living God is among you, and that he will *without fail* drive out from before you the Canaanites, and the Hittites, and the Hivites, and the Perizzites, and the Girgashites, and the Amorites, and the Jebusites. Josh. 3:10

We see this picture of sanctification as a time of preparation. Sanctification has two major parts: one is separation from worldly things, and the other is a separation unto God. If you knew that Jesus was coming tomorrow, would you begin to do some things in your life that you haven't done up until this time in order to be ready? You would prepare yourself, you would sanctify yourself. There would be certain things that just wouldn't matter anymore. They were all right as pursuits previously, but under the circumstances those pursuits are totally inappropriate. That is what Joshua was saying here — "Sanctify yourselves for tomorrow God will work wonders among you."

There is a time of preparation, and in order for that preparation to take place in us, we need to have a more extreme separation unto Him, **because we are entering a time of the greatest expression of God's grace and power that the world has ever known!** This is part of what the trumpet sound means by the calling of the assembly.

Journeying of the Camp

There is something else that is meant by this trumpet sound. The latter part of verse 2 of Numbers 10 says, "and for the journeying of the camps." Every time God wanted to move, He would cause the cloud to lift and begin to journey, and Israel would break camp and follow the cloud. Whenever the cloud began to move, those who were in charge of the trumpet would sound it, announcing that it was time to go on. We can't camp here any longer. It's time to move into whatever God is leading us to.

What we have seen concerning the meaning of this call is that it is a call to:

(1) Go on and keep the feast of the Day of Atonement and Tabernacles, which will mean a call to go on to completion and maturity.

(2) Come out of tribal loyalties and to find a loyalty to the Body of Christ, in which the Baptism of the Holy Spirit in this Charismatic Renewal has been a catalyst.

This means that we no longer harp on a particular doctrinal pattern but come to the truth of Christ in His fullness, no matter what it is. If our traditions have not borne up the truth of God's Word, they must be laid aside. We must find that our loyalty is no longer just denominational. This doesn't mean you cannot belong to a denomination; you need to belong to something in order to relate and work together corporately. Your denomination is as your tribal family. However, you should not be denominationally oriented. Your orientation should be to the entire Body of Christ.

The journeying of the camps also means that there is to be a gathering unto the Lord one by one. We see this prophetically in Isaiah 27:12–13 as it has been fulfilled in the nation of Israel and its parallel being fulfilled in the church:

> And it shall come to pass in that day, that the Lord shall beat off from the channel of the river unto the stream of Egypt, and you shall be gathered one by one, O ye children of Israel. And it shall come to pass in that day, that the great trumpet shall be blown, and they shall come which were ready to perish in the land of Assyria, and the outcasts in the land of Egypt, and shall worship the Lord in the holy mount at Jerusalem. Is. 27:12–13

Preparation of the people for war

> And if you go to war in your land against the enemy that oppresses you, then you shall blow an alarm with the trumpets; and you shall be remembered before the Lord your God, and you shall be saved from your enemies. Numbers 10:9

One of the great things that the church has not understood is spiritual warfare. As we go to war, we have to recognize that most Christians in recent generations haven't understood that there is spiritual warfare. Some have begun to realize that there is a genuine spiritual warfare taking place; however, most of them don't even know what it's all about, let alone how to fight it effectively. They don't have their weapons together, they don't know how to go to war, they don't understand the enemy's tactics, they don't understand his objectives and methods, they don't understand God's objectives and methods, and they don't know how to take the victory as a result. Part of the trumpet sound is a **call for the people to be prepared for war.**

I see four levels of Christian experience. The first level is when you receive your salvation. The second level is receiving the Baptism of the Holy Spirit; along with this you find the release of the gifts of the Spirit in your life, the operation of walking in the Spirit and the working of the Spirit in your inner man. Third, you go on to sonship, where you learn to be an overcomer over your fallen nature; you develop some stability, consistency and victory in your life. *Then* you can begin to understand the fourth plane, the warfare plane. Why not before? If you go out to war and can't stand in victory or walk with God having learned how to abide in the Spirit and come under the discipline of the Spirit, you will be easily overthrown by the enemy. Not that the enemy is that smart; he does the same things over and over again, but we are ignorant. It's not that the enemy is that powerful, but we're so sloppy in our walk before God that we leave ourselves vulnerable so that he can easily overthrow us. So we have to learn to overcome before we can go to war in order to find ourselves effective.

The crusade ministry is warfare, it's invasion into the enemy's territory. It's nuclear warfare in the Spirit. We find a stronghold that the Lord takes us to, set up our artillery, get a battle plan, go in and declare war on the enemy and blast him out of there! After it's over we rejoice in the victory. But we have a saying: THE ENEMY WILL WORK IN EVERY PLACE THAT YOU ASSUME. The enemy will be hard at work on every little detail in your personal walk, your battle plan and your prayer life that you may have overlooked and not committed to the Lord. And he wins if you leave enough places open — not because he's so powerful or so smart, but because you failed to be what you needed to be to go to war.

What is warfare like?

> And there was war in heaven: Michael and his angels fought against the dragon; and the dragon fought and his angels, and prevailed not; neither was their place found any more in heaven. And the great dragon was cast out, that old serpent, called the Devil, and Satan, which deceives the whole world: he was cast out into

the earth, and his angels were cast out with him. And I heard a loud voice saying in heaven, Now is come salvation, and strength, and the kingdom of our God, and the power of his Christ: for the accuser of our brethren is cast down, which accused them before our God day and night. And they overcame him by the blood of the Lamb, and by the word of their testimony; and they loved not their lives unto the death.
Rev. 12:7–11

I know of only one genuine commentary on the meaning of this passage, and it is in the Gospel of Luke. The 70 had been sent out by the Lord to heal the sick and proclaim that the Kingdom of God had come near to them.

And the seventy returned again with joy, saying, Lord, even the devils are subject unto us through thy name. And Jesus said unto them, I beheld Satan as lightning fall from heaven. Behold I give unto you power to tread on serpents and scorpions, and over all the power of the enemy: and nothing shall by any means hurt you. Notwithstanding in this rejoice not, that the spirits are subject unto you; but rather rejoice, because your names are written in heaven. Luke 10:17–20

THE POWER AND THE AUTHORITY THAT JESUS GAVE TO HIS DISCIPLES, MANIFESTED IN PREACHING THE GOSPEL TO THE UNSAVED AND HEALING THE SICK, WAS COMMENTED UPON BY JESUS AS SEEING SATAN CAST OUT OF HEAVEN AS LIGHTNING. *Warfare deals with bringing down the enemy's strongholds in heavenly places.* Ephesians tells us that we wrestle not with flesh and blood but with spiritual wickedness and principalities and powers in heavenly places. When the victory is taken in the spirit world, something is manifest in the natural world.

This is warfare, this is battle, and **the sound of the trumpet is to call the church to prepare for spiritual war. As a result of this warfare there will come the greatest manifestation of God's power, His grace, miracles, healing and the salvation of the lost that the world has ever seen! I John 3:8 says that the Son was manifested to destroy the works of the devil. The trumpet sounds an alarm of the judgment to come upon the enemy's world.**

Along this line, certain prophecies should be examined. Joel is the prophet of the ministry of the Day of Trumpets.

Blow ye the trumpet in Zion, and sound an alarm in my holy mountain: let all the inhabitants of the land tremble: for the day of the Lord comes, for it is near at hand; a day of darkness and of gloominess, a day of clouds and of thick darkness, as the morning spread upon the mountains: a great people and a strong; there has not been ever the like, neither shall be any more after it, even to the years of many generations. A fire devours before them; and behind them a flame burns: the land is as the garden of Eden before them, and behind them a desolate wilderness; yea, and nothing shall escape them. Joel 2:1-3

A cross-reference is pictured in Isaiah 13:

The noise of a multitude in the mountains, like as of a great people; a tumultuous noise of the kingdom of nations gathered together: the Lord of hosts musters the host of the battle. They come from a far country, from the end of heaven, even the Lord, and the weapons of his indignation, to destroy the whole land. Isa. 13:4-5

Judgment is to come. Those who understand the Kingdom of God in the Scripture learn that before every period of God's judgment was a preceding period of God's grace, and the greater the judgment that was to come the greater the period of grace that preceded it. A very obvious example is the Lord Jesus Christ coming in the incarnation to Israel. Before He was rejected and crucified, He stood above the city of Jerusalem and wept and cried, "O Jerusalem, Jerusalem, how many times I would have gathered you under my arms as a mother hen with chicks under her wings, but ye would not. Therefore, you shall be desolate." Therefore, judgment will come. They crucified Him, and within a generation Titus led the Roman armies through Jerusalem and so leveled the city that nothing was left.

The judgment that follows the final outpouring of God's Spirit at the end of the Church Age is against the rule of the antichrist kingdom before the Millennial reign. It is part of the meaning of the trumpet sound.

If we go on to understand this meaning, we must understand that **the heavens and the earth are going to be shaken. Everything that can be shaken will be shaken in this period of time.**

Multitudes, multitudes in the valley of decision: for the day of the Lord is near in the valley of decision. The sun and the moon shall be darkened, and the stars shall withdraw their shining. The Lord also shall roar out of Zion, and utter his voice from Jerusalem; and the heavens and the earth shall shake: but the Lord will be the hope of his people, and the strength of the children of Israel. So shall ye know that I am the Lord your God dwelling in Zion, my holy mountain: then shall Jerusalem be holy, and there shall no strangers pass through her any more. Joel 3:14-17

This is a prophecy of a time of decision, followed by judgment for those who reject the Lord. A judgment can be very positive if you're on the right side, but if you're not it can be very, very devastating. God is going to pour out of His Spirit in an extremely solemn way.

A call to holiness

Also in the day of your gladness, and in your solemn days, and in the beginnings of your months, ye shall blow with the trumpets over your burnt offerings, and over the sacrifices of your peace offerings; that they may be to you for a memorial before your God: I am the Lord your God. Num. 10:10

These solemn days are the feast day periods. On the feast day of Trumpets they blew the trumpets announcing that on the tenth of that seventh month would be the Feast of the Day of Atonement, their most holy day, in which there would be the sacrifice for sins and the sins of Israel would be removed. Trumpets is a call to go on to the Day of Atonement.

What does that mean to you and me? It means that there must be a judgment in us, for the Scripture says that judgment begins at the house of God. That is what is meant in Isaiah 58 about those who sought Him daily, delighted in His ways, sought His justice and didn't forsake His ordinances. **There is a level of repentance and sanctification that must go so deep in us that sin in our life is fully judged, that we allow it to be fully dealt with by the Cross, that we might be freed from it by the power of the Spirit.**

The meaning of Pentecost included a greater harvest to follow – the fruit of the Spirit as well as the fruit of souls. But we haven't seen that harvest, and it is what must come to our lives. John the Baptist preached that every tree that does not bring forth fruit will be cut down and burned in preparation for the coming of the Lord. According to the prophecy at the end of Malachi concerning Elijah and its amplification in John the Baptist's life, John's ministry speaks of the end of the Church Age. There will be that kind of ministry before the return of Jesus Christ and every tree that does not bring forth fruit will be hewn down. Are you a fruitful Christian? If you're not bearing fruit in your life, you will be broken off. Jesus said it in John 15: "I am the vine and you are the branches. Every branch that brings forth not fruit will be cut off and burned." If you bring forth fruit, you are pruned so you can bring forth more fruit. Listen to the cry of the prophet Joel as he sounds this part of the message, remembering that "field" is a type of the world:

> The field is wasted, the land mourns; for the corn is wasted: the new wine is dried up, the oil languishes. Be ye ashamed, O ye husbandmen; howl, O ye vinedressers, for the wheat and for the barley; because the harvest of the field is perished. The vine is dried up, and the fig tree languishes; the pomegranate tree, the palm tree also, and the apple tree, even all the trees of the field, are withered: because joy is withered away from the sons of men. Joel 1:10–12

Pentecost lost its meaning because the harvest failed. *The Baptism of the Holy Spirit in your life will lose its meaning if you don't go on to have a spiritual harvest of Christian character and effectiveness in touching a lost world.* I have seen many churches that have not moved on and they've dried up on the vine. They have the outward form but the life is gone because they had no fruit. They didn't go on to Tabernacles. It isn't enough to have a little blessing — *you must understand the purpose of the blessing.* It isn't enough to have the outpouring of the Holy Spirit, for God to slay you in the power of the Spirit, to give you a message in prophecy or tongues, to heal you of your cancer or to intervene supernaturally in your affairs. **IT'S NOT ENOUGH IF IT DOESN'T CHANGE YOUR CHARACTER. When the Fruit Inspector comes and finds no fruit, there won't be any excuse. He is not a respecter of persons. Either we allow the Holy Spirit to deal with us and change us where we**

need to be changed, or we will be cut off. *That doesn't mean that you are perfect now. It does mean that you are real enough in your walk with God that you're allowing Him to expose areas that are contrary to His Word; you're not hiding and excusing them or sweeping them under the rug or procrastinating in them, but you are dealing with them* by saying, "God, I recognize it, I acknowledge it, I ask your forgiveness, teach me your ways, help me to grow that I might change." As you look back over your life, you consistently see areas that have been changed by the grace of God's Spirit. If you are not changing, then you need to know that you're in spiritual trouble and God has an answer for you if you want it. If you are changing, then you are receiving the message of Trumpets.

We are to deal with the fact that the harvest field is perishing. Let us look at this on two levels:

(1) The fruit of the Spirit, Christian character developing in your life. Is your life strongly developed enough in the Lord that people are seeing the changes and eating the fruit of it? Are there character changes happening in your life that reflect the character of Christ?

(2) The world is wasted. My in-laws are farmers of fruit. If I go up to see my brother-in-law during harvest time, I find that he is unavailable. He will be up by daylight and will be home when it's dark. He will hit the bed, get up in the morning while it's still dark and work until dark every day until the harvest is in. Why? *The fruit, when it's ripe, will not wait.* If it gets too ripe, it falls off the tree, hits the ground and is lost forever. When the season is right, he will get everyone he can to go over there and reap the harvest, and they will work from daylight until dark every day until the harvest is brought in. If they don't, the fruit drops on the ground and rots.

That is what Joel is saying: THE FIELD IS WASTED. In spite of the fact that more souls are being born into the Kingdom per day than at any time in church history, the world population is growing percentage-wise faster than the church. In spite of all that God is doing and as wonderful as it is, we have to face the fact that the Body of Christ around the world as a whole is not doing the job. We are failing to reap our generation, the harvest is falling on the ground and is wasted. **PRAY YE THEREFORE THE LORD OF HARVEST THAT HE**

MIGHT SEND FORTH LABORERS UNTO THE HARVEST, FOR THE HARVEST IS PLENTEOUS BUT THE LABORERS ARE FEW.

How much is enough for you? What are you living for? When it's all over and done, are the goals you have been living for worthy of a lifetime of living? Are you going to be able to look back and say, I invested my talents, my abilities and my resources to reach my generation? The fact is that 90% of the Body of Christ in America today does not regularly lead people to Jesus. That means 10% of the Body of Christ is alive and functioning and 90% is asleep, or half-dead. Whatever excuse we might use, the fact is the harvest is ripe, the laborers are few and there is more that needs to be done than is being done.

The trumpet sound is to awaken us to the harvest and to go on to Atonement. What happens at Atonement? The sins of selfcenteredness, the misuses of our talents and our life, and the misdirection of our priorities are adjusted and changed and removed from our life so that the fullness of Christ might come in us and through us and the harvest be reaped. *IT IS TO SOUND AN ALARM. WE ARE IN A TIME OF WAR.* WE HAVE TO GO TO THE BATTLE, WE HAVE TO GET PREPARED, WE HAVE TO GET SANCTIFIED. GOD IS GOING TO WORK WITH US, HE'S GOING TO WORK WONDERS AMONG US, BUT SOUND THE ALARM AND LET THE PEOPLE COME OUT OF THEIR TRIBES, OUT OF THEIR TENTS, GATHER TOGETHER AS ONE AND BE PREPARED FOR WHAT GOD WILL DO AMONG US!

Those who have ears to hear in the day in which we live recognize that the restoration of Israel, the Six Day War, the Yom Kippur War, the peace initiative, Jerusalem coming under the government of Israel and the Charismatic Renewal are prophetic fulfillments of God's Word which tell us the meaning of the sounding of the Day of Trumpets. It is a sign of the season that *now* is the time we should hear the alarm and rally to the call.

> Blow the trumpet in Zion, sanctify a fast, call a solemn assembly: Gather the people, sanctify the congregation, assemble the elders, gather the children, and those that suck the breasts: let the bridegroom go forth of his chamber, and the bride out of her closet.

Let the priests, the ministers of the Lord, weep between the porch and the altar, and let them say, Spare thy people, O Lord, and give not thine heritage to reproach, that the heathen should rule over them: *wherefore should they say among the people, Where is their God?* Joel 2:15–17

Do you hear the accusation of the world? WHERE IS THEIR GOD? The world looks at the church that has been without the power and character and they say, WHERE IS THEIR GOD? **There is only one answer: the church is to rally to the trumpet call that they might stand in the anointing and the power of the Holy Spirit.** They are to be like Elisha when he took Elijah's mantle and smote the waters and said, "Where is the Lord God of Elijah?" and the power of God was manifest.

We need to rally to the battle, we need the power of God! We can see the devil be cast out of heaven as lightning, see people healed and delivered, see the glory of God manifested! We have seen only a little trickle of what God wants to do. This is part of the trumpet cry, and the point is that this feast has never been kept before in the history of the world. This generation, the one in which we live, is the first one to ever keep it and may be the only one that will. We are called to go on.

WE CAN'T PLAY CHURCH ANY LONGER. THE HOUR HAS COME WHEN WE MUST MOVE INTO GOD AND HIS DIVINE PURPOSE AND GET SERIOUS AND LET GOD DEAL WITH US. WE MUST SAY, "ALL RIGHT, GOD, THIS SCRIPTURE SAYS THESE SIGNS SHALL FOLLOW THEM WHO BELIEVE; GREATER WORKS SHALL THEY DO; I CAN OVERCOME THESE SINS IN MY LIFE; I CAN HEAR YOUR VOICE AND BE LED BY YOUR SPIRIT. I CAN FIND THESE KINDS OF THINGS COME TO PASS AND I WANT THEM. I'M NO LONGER GOING TO READ THEM AND SAY, 'OH, THAT'S WONDERFUL,' CLOSE THE BOOK AND DO MY OWN THING. I DON'T KNOW HOW THIS THING IS GOING TO HAPPEN, BUT I'M GOING TO TRUST YOU TO TEACH ME, TO LEAD ME, TO DEAL WITH ME, THAT I MIGHT PROGRESS IN RIGHTEOUSNESS, THAT I MIGHT PROGRESS IN KNOWLEDGE, THAT I MIGHT BE BETTER QUALIFIED FOR YOU TO HONOR MY LIFE WITH DIVINE INTERVENTION IN ORDER TO TOUCH A LOST AND DYING

WORLD AND TO SEE YOUR PURPOSES COMPLETED IN THE EARTH."

Father, help us to hear the cry of your Holy Spirit in this hour, and grant to us the grace that we need in order to respond. Stir our spirits and awaken us out of our slumber that we might move with you into the greatest hour the church has ever known. Amen.

THE DAY OF ATONEMENT

The Feast of the Day of Trumpets on the first day of the seventh month announced the Day of Atonement ten days later. This event took place once a year in Israel's history in order to deal with the atoning of sin. Sacrifices were accepted or rejected for the annual cleansing of the people, the sanctuary and the nation before God. These events were prophetic of what would happen to Christ when He was crucified as our lamb, and also of events that would occur in Israel's future.

This was the most solemn of feast days. It is called Yom Kippur among the Israelis today. On Yom Kippur in 1973 there was an invasion into Israel orchestrated by the Soviet Union with Egypt and Syria, as discussed earlier. Prophecies in Ezekiel concerning Gog and Magog speak of the people who live in the area above the Black Sea, which is Russia. Other countries mentioned in the prophecies were Persia, which today is Iran, and Ethiopia. They are all to be part of an attack against Israel which is a pre-Tribulation, pre-Rapture, pre-Second Coming of Christ event.

What was the Yom Kippur War in 1973 but a dress rehearsal? Iran at that time was pro-Israel; today, it is not. Ethiopia at that time was pro-Israel; today, it is not. Egypt at that time was one of the major pincers in that war against Israel, and that country would not be in the battle if it took place today. Events are surely moving to set up Gog and Magog.

Each one of these events is significant. Just before the Yom Kippur War, on the Day of the Feast of Trumpets, Time Magazine carried on the front page a story concerning a Levitical priest flown by helicopter to Mt. Sinai to blow a trumpet. Israel had become restored as a nation. The Yom Kippur war followed and these events signally focussed the attention of the world on the Day of Atonement in Israel, their most holy day, the day on which they were attacked. This is because God is calling the church to keep this feast.

What does this really mean? It means that full and complete atonement has been made by Jesus on Calvary, and **the church that has never fully appropriated or fully received all that the atonement has provided is to come into this fullness.** In other words, *for the church, the Day of Atonement* *represents the experiential appropriation of the atonement. For Israel, it is the receiving of their Messiah, who is Christ.* These events of the feasts are not always simultaneous for the church and Israel. Israel's original Passover was not on the Passover for the church, which was when Christ was crucified, but it was prophetic for Israel. We must remember that the Day of Atonement does not bring the same truths as Passover. At Passover the blood is applied and righteousness is imputed to us — that is when we're born again. At Day of Atonement righteousness is implemented in our life in its fullness. Let me show you what this means for Israel.

During the Church Age Israel has been blinded to a degree because of their rejection of Christ (Rom. 11:25), but through the Tribulation period they will recognize that they have rejected their Messiah. In one day the remaining Israeli survivors of the Tribulation will receive their Messiah and Christ will part the skies and return with His saints (Rom. 11:26; I Thess. 3:13). This means that we, as His saints, will have to already be where He is in order to return with Him. There are three comings of Christ: the first one is the incarnation, the second one when He comes *for* his church, and the third one when He comes *with* His church. When He comes for His church we meet Him in the air; when He comes with His church He plants His feet on the Mount of Olives and the Battle of Armageddon takes place. He will destroy the antichrist and his armies that come against Israel and the Millennial kingdom will be set up. It is this coming of the Lord as the deliverer of Israel that brings to fulfillment the Day of Atonement for them.

> For I would not, brethren, that ye should be ignorant of this mystery, lest ye should be wise in your own conceits; that blindness in part is happened to Israel, until the fullness of the Gentiles be come in. And so all Israel shall be saved: as it is written, There shall come out of Sion the Deliverer, and shall turn away ungodliness from Jacob: For this is my covenant unto them, when I shall take away their sins.
> Rom. 11:25–27

What is the sign of the end of the time for the Gentile? Jesus said that Jerusalem would be trodden down of the Gentiles until the time of the Gentiles be fulfilled (Luke 21:24). In 1967, during the Six Day War, Old Jerusalem came under the government of Israel as captured territory of war for the first time in a couple thousand of years. In August of 1980 the Knesset, the ruling government of Israel, decided to make Old Jerusalem their official capital, no longer to be just a captured territory. Any way you look at it, this prophecy is being fulfilled in our day. The church is now living in the overlap period between the end of the Church Age and the ushering in of the Millennium! Every major dispensation had an overlap period. You see it between the law and the church — when John the Baptist was ministering and Christ's ministry was born. The overlap takes place in a generation, and we are the most privileged people to ever walk on the face of the earth because we're born in this generation.

> For behold the stone that I have laid before Joshua; upon one stone shall be seven eyes: behold, I will engrave the graving thereof, saith the Lord of hosts, and I will remove the iniquity of that land *in one day.* Zech. 3:9

This is the Day of Atonement prophetically fulfilled for Israel. Passover, Unleavened Bread, Firstfruits and Pentecost were fulfilled in a single day, and the Day of Atonement will be fulfilled in a single day. Christ was crucified at Passover, buried at Unleavened Bread, rose on Firstfruits, the outpouring of the Holy Spirit occurred at Pentecost, and the blowing of the Day of Trumpets (Israel restored as a nation) took place in a single day.

For the church there is also a unique application of these truths.

> And grieve not the holy Spirit of God, whereby ye are *sealed unto the day of redemption.* Eph. 4:30

We are sealed by the Holy Spirit of promise with a seal that is to find its fulfillment in a day called the Day of Redemption, the Day of Atonement.

Consistency of interpretation will show that as each of the feast days was a 24-hour period in the history of Israel and the church, so it must be with the Day of Atonement. Every feast, once it was initiated, has remained open to all who would enter in as far as its spiritual truth and experience are concerned. For instance, anyone who wants to keep the Feast of Passover can do so from the point that it was fulfilled when Christ was crucified.

And the Lord spoke to Moses, saying, Also on the tenth day of this seventh month there shall be a day of atonement: it shall be a holy convocation to you: and you shall afflict your souls, and offer an offering made by fire unto the Lord. And you shall do no work in that same day: for it is a day of atonement, to make an atonement for you before the Lord your God. For whatsoever soul it be that shall not be afflicted in that same day, he shall be cut off from among his people. And whatsoever soul it be that doeth any work in that same day, the same soul will I destroy from among his people. You shall do no manner of work: it shall be a statute for ever throughout your generation in all your dwellings. Lev. 23:26–31

Then shalt thou cause *the trumpet of the jubilee to sound* on the tenth day of the seventh month, *in the day of atonement* shall ye make the trumpet sound throughout all your land. Lev. 25:9

The year of jubilee was a year of release and occurred every seven years. In that year all slaves and prisoners were set free; all who owed debts had them canceled; there was to be no work and no farming of the land; and because the land was given by God as an inheritance when they came into Canaan, every family would go back to that portion of land that had been given to them and it would become theirs once again. They could never permanently lose their land. **This has a significance of being released from the consequences of sin while possessing our full inheritance. In the year of jubilee none of these blessings could be received until after the festivities of the Day of Atonement, and there are some things that we will not possess until that day is kept by the church.**

It was a holy convocation, which meant that no work was to be done from evening to evening. Israel had to cease from their own works and rest in the work of the atonement. If they did not, they were cut off. They had to rest in the work of the high priest in sanctuary service. For the believer, this means that *we are to rest* in Christ's finished work. *Like all holy convocations or sabbaths*, it means that we cease from our own labors. That doesn't mean that we don't wash dishes, but IT DOES MEAN THAT WE CEASE FROM ADAM, WE CEASE

FROM LIVING FROM THE LIFE THAT WAS GIVEN US BY CREATION AND ABIDE IN CHRIST, REST IN HIM AND LIVE BY HIS LIFE. In other words, this holy convocation in its fullness means that we are in a place of abiding and walking in the Spirit, and if we walk in the Spirit we will not fulfill the lust of the flesh. **THERE IS A TIME AND PLACE OF VICTORY THAT IS SO COMPLETE THAT YOU WILL ABIDE IN THE SPIRIT AND BECAUSE OF THAT ABIDING IN THE SPIRIT, YOU WILL NOT FULFILL THE LUST OF THE FLESH, YOU WILL HAVE TOTAL VICTORY!**

The Day of Atonement was the only feast day that was one of fasting. It was a time of dealing with the flesh, a time of discipline to bring the natural man under the government of the Spirit of God. It was a day of soul affliction. The Israelite would humble himself in repentance in seeking God and accepted the dealings of God in his life for sin. As we come into this period, we must recognize that it is a time when God begins to really deal with and change sin patterns in our life. The parallel in the New Testament is what we read every time we have communion: if we would judge ourselves we would not be judged (I Cor. 11). A time comes when there is a willful bringing of those things which are not right before God and allowing Him to deal with them and to make them right in our life.

The Day of Atonement was held on the tenth day of the seventh month. Seven is the number of fullness in the Bible, the number of completeness and perfection. Ten is the number of testing, trial and responsibility before God. There were ten days of preparation from Trumpets to Atonement, and all of Israel was responsible to prepare themselves for the great Day of Atonement. The fact that we have seen the keeping of the Feast of the Day of Trumpets in church history means that every Christian who is walking with God and who is in tune with what God is doing today is in the process of preparing to keep the Day of Atonement.

There are several scriptures which show how the number ten deals with testing.

> Prove thy servants, I beseech thee, ten days; and let them give us pulse to eat, and water to drink.
> Dan. 1:12

Daniel, Shadrach, Meshach and Abednego would not eat of the king's meat offered to idols. They were not going to violate the law concerning diet and they were to be proven ten days.

> Fear none of those things which thou shalt suffer: behold, the devil shall cast some of you into prison, that ye may be tried; and ye shall have tribulation ten days: be thou faithful unto death, and I will give thee a crown of life. Rev. 2:10

The law came with ten commandments dealing with our responsibility before God, and certainly the law was a test for mankind.

It is a time of testing and preparation. If we do not recognize this, we will misunderstand what is happening in the days in which we are living right now. **The testing is meant to bring us to a place of preparedness to keep the fullness of the Day of Atonement.**

The Day of Atonement ceremonies are very interesting:

> And the Lord spoke to Moses after the death of the two sons of Aaron, when they offered before the Lord, and died; and the Lord said unto Moses, Speak unto Aaron thy brother, that he come not at all times into the holy place within the vail before the mercy seat, which is upon the ark; that he die not: for I will appear in the cloud upon the mercy seat. Lev. 16:1–2

> And he shall take a censer full of burning coals of fire from off the altar before the Lord, and his hands full of sweet incense beaten small, and bring it within the vail: And he shall put the incense upon the fire before the Lord, that the cloud of the incense may cover the mercy seat that is upon the testimony, that he die not. Lev. 16:12–13

On the Day of Atonement the lamb was slain and Aaron had to go into the Holy of Holies and sprinkle the blood.

> Which had the golden censer, and the ark of the covenant overlaid round about with gold, wherein was the golden pot that had manna, and Aaron's rod that budded, and the tables of the covenant. Heb. 9:4

Only on this day would the High Priest go within the veil into the Holiest of All. The incense and its ingredients always speak of prayer and worship in the Scripture.

Let my prayer be set forth before thee as incense; and the lifting up of my hands as the evening sacrifice. Ps. 141:2

And when he had taken the book, the four beasts and four and twenty elders fell down before the Lamb, having every one of them harps, and golden vials full of odors, which are the prayers of saints. Rev. 5:8

And when he had opened the seventh seal, there was silence in heaven about the space of half an hour. And I saw the seven angels which stood before God: and to them were given seven trumpets. And another angel came and stood at the altar, having a golden censer; and there was given unto him much incense, that he should offer it with the prayers of all saints upon the golden altar which was before the throne. And the smoke of the incense, which came with the prayers of the saints, ascended up before God out of the angel's hand. And the angel took the censer, and filled it with fire of the altar, and cast it into the earth: and there were voices, and thunderings, and lightnings and an earthquake. Rev. 8:1–5

Christ is the High Priest before the throne, the mediator of a better covenant, and our prayers are the means by which we have entrance. There is something represented by the Day of Atonement in that it is **a time of renewed prayer and intercession.**

Christ, our forerunner, has entered first within the veil and we have access through Him with worship and prayer. You're not really entering in to what God has available if you are not developing your prayer life and your worship. You cannot come this far without keeping the other feasts, but *if you're going on within the veil and into that place where you meet with the glory of God, then it must come with prayer and worship.*

As we go on, we find that there was to be the washing of water at this time.

He shall put on the holy linen coat, and he shall have the linen breeches upon his flesh, and shall be girded with a linen girdle, and with the linen mitre shall he be attired: these are holy garments: therefore shall he wash his flesh in water, and so put them on. Lev. 16:4

And he shall wash his flesh with water in the holy place, and put on his garments, and come forth, and offer his burnt offering, and the burnt offering of the people, and make an atonement for himself, and for the people. Lev. 16:24

Husbands, love your wives, even as Christ also loved the church, and gave himself for it; that he might sanctify and cleanse it with the washing of water by the word, that he might present it to himself a glorious church, not having spot, or wrinkle, or any such thing; but that it should be holy and without blemish.
Eph. 5:25–27

At the entrance to the Holy Place in Moses' Tabernacle, to which Leviticus is referring, they had what was called the brazen laver containing water. The priest had to cut the throats of lambs, catch the blood, roast the sacrifice, and needed to get washed up before he went into the Holy Place or the Holy of Holies. The brazen laver was polished to such an extent that you could see yourself in it.

Wherefore lay apart all filthiness and superfluity of naughtiness, and receive with meekness the engrafted word, which is able to save your souls. But be ye doers of the word, and not hearers only, deceiving your own selves. For if any be a hearer of the word, and not a doer, he is like unto a man beholding his natural face in a glass: For he beholdeth himself, and goes his way, and straightaway forgets what manner of man he was. But whoso looks into the perfect law of liberty, and continues therein, he being not a forgetful hearer, but a doer of the work, this man shall be blessed in his deed. James 1:21–25

It isn't enough to look and see; it isn't enough to be a hearer only and be able to understand in your mind and share it with someone else. You don't wash by just dipping your hands in the water or looking at it, you must apply it. The Word must be applied in your life. The washing of water means being doers of the Word, where Christ through the Spirit of God takes the Word, applies it to our life and shows us where our life is not conformable to His ways. As a result, there is an adjustment that must be made, there is a cleansing, there is a removing of the blemishes or the shortcomings, the removing of the spots, the little places in our life that are not as they should be. *The Word of God applied makes us so that we are without spot or wrinkle or blemish or any such thing.* The Day of Atonement involves the washing of water, the Word applied so that righteousness is implemented in our lives.

Are you beginning to get a feeling for what this feast means? We are to be doers of the Word. Righteousness implemented, not imputed as at Passover. When you say, "I ask you, Jesus, to come into my life and be Savior." He says, "Yes, I forgive you, my blood has cleansed you, you are standing before me just as if you were perfect, it's imputed unto you for righteousness. BUT, *between this point and the time you're coming home, that righteousness is going to be worked into your life."* You go to Unleavened Bread and bury the old man; Firstfruits and rise in newness of life; receive the Baptism of the Holy Spirit at Pentecost and begin to get some power; on to Trumpets and come out of self-centeredness and into the Body; and then to warfare and the Day of Atonement, where you find a full appropriation of Calvary and victory over sin in your life!

> And Aaron shall come into the tabernacle of the congregation, and shall put off the linen garments, which he put on when he went into the holy place, and shall leave them there. Lev. 16:23

The High Priest would wear garments embroidered with gold and jewels. However, on the Day of Atonement he would take those garments off and put on a fine linen garment to go into the Holy of Holies.

> And take thou unto thee Aaron thy brother, and his sons with him, from among the children of Israel, that he may minister unto me in the priest's office. And thou shalt make holy garments for Aaron thy brother for glory and for beauty. Exo. 28:1-2

> And these are the garments which they shall make; a breastplate, and an ephod, and a robe, and a broidered coat, a mitre, and a girdle: and they shall make holy garments for Aaron thy brother, and his sons, that he may minister unto me in the priest's office. And they shall take gold, and blue, and purple, and scarlet, and fine linen. Exo. 28:3-5

The representation of the plain linen garment for Christ is quite clear. You see it in Philippians Chapter 2, where Jesus thought it not robbery to be called equal with God but emptied and humbled Himself and became as a man, and being found as a man He became obedient as a servant even unto the death of the cross. *He left His glory in heaven to walk among us as a man,* but He was perfect and sinless in His humanity. The fine linen garment speaks of His sinless humanity. What does it mean for the believer?

I will greatly rejoice in the Lord, my soul shall be joyful in my God; for he has clothed me with the garments of salvation, he has covered me with the robe of righteousness, as a bridegroom decks himself with ornaments, and as a bride adorns herself with her jewels. Isa. 61:10

Let us be glad and rejoice, and give honor to him: for the marriage of the Lamb is come, and his wife has made herself ready. And to her was granted that she should be arrayed in fine linen, clean and white: for the fine linen is the righteousness of saints. Rev. 19:7–8

The literal Greek says it was granted to her to array herself in fine linen. "Righteousness" is translated as the righteous conduct of saints. The righteous conduct is a reflection of choice; choice is a reflection of the place of the will; and the will is the expression of character. Righteous conduct is another way of saying Christ's character. **The fine linen, clean and white, is then representative of the character of Christ in the believer, the garment of the Bride.** Because some have not allowed God to develop their character, they will not be dressed in the wedding garment.

In order to go into the place within the veil where the fullness and glory of God was, there had to be a development. We see it with the washing of water by the Word, and we see it again with the fine linen, clean and white, the righteousness and character of God developed in us.

And he shall take of the blood of the bullock, and sprinkle it with his finger upon the mercy seat eastward; and before the mercy seat shall he sprinkle of the blood with his finger seven times. Lev. 16:14

This speaks of the perfection that the blood of Jesus will bring to His church in the end time. At Passover the blood was put on the doorposts and on the lintel — righteousness imputed but not implemented. At Pentecost the blood was sprinkled out towards the people, who had a certain cleansing, and on the book of the covenant — illumination in the Book through the Baptism of the Holy Spirit. We come to this last feast and the blood is sprinkled seven times on the mercy seat. **The Day of Atonement in the church, then, will be the fullest manifestation of the power of the blood of Jesus Christ.**

The blood and the Spirit are one, because the life is in the blood, according to Leviticus, and the Spirit is life. You cannot separate them in the Scripture. *Everything* that you want to have in Calvary comes on the basis of the blood of Jesus; everything that you have in God has its foundation in the blood of Jesus. When we talk about sprinkling seven times on the mercy seat, dealing with where the blood atonement was made, that speaks of the completion of the atonement, ALL THAT WAS PURCHASED AND MADE AVAILABLE BY THE BLOOD BEING MANIFEST EXPERIENTIALLY. There is here the fullest manifestation of the power of the blood of Jesus ever known. **It will bring the church to completion by making an end of sin, iniquity, transgression and uncleanness.**

In order to understand the New Testament interpretation of this, we need to understand the nature of victory over sin which the Scripture promises. It is not our ability that will enable us to fully appropriate victory over sin. It will not be our holiness that is appropriated, for the righteousness of man is as filthy rags to God. If you had holiness in yourself, you would not need Calvary. Your created life cannot be made perfect; it has been destroyed forever by sin. That is why there must be a death, because the wages of sin is death. Christ experienced that death for us on Calvary so that by the operation of grace, we can lay down our sin–cursed life and in exchange receive the perfect life of Christ by the miracle of the new birth. *Christ is our righteousness.* You and I have not yet seen the fullness of Christ in our own personal life, but that is the meaning of the Day of Atonement. The life of Christ is growing and developing in you, it is not stagnant. **You are changing from glory to glory and every time He moves**

on you by His Spirit, every time He deals with you in the Word, every time He brings you to genuine repentance, every time He opens your understanding with new revelation, every time He brings you a spiritual victory, you are changed and that change is more into the likeness of Christ. The Scripture says that the path of the just (those who are obedient to the light that they have) is as a shining light that will shine more and more unto the perfect day (Prov. 4:18).

> And this shall be a statute forever unto you: that in the seventh month, on the tenth day of the month, you shall afflict your souls, and do no work at all, whether it be one of your own country, or a stranger that sojourns among you: For on that day shall the priest make an atonement for you, to cleanse you, that *you may be clean from all your sins before the Lord.* It shall be a sabbath of rest unto you, and you shall afflict your souls, by a statute forever. Lev. 16:29–31

Anything that is forever has its fulfillment in the everlasting covenant, the New Covenant.

> *Be ye therefore perfect,* even as your Father which is in heaven is perfect. Matt. 5:48

> That they all may be one; as thou, Father, art in me, and I in thee, that they also may be one in us: that the world may believe that you have sent me. And the glory which you gave me I have given them; that they may be one, even as we are one: I in them, and thou in me, *that they may be made perfect in one;* and that the world may know that you have sent me, and has loved them, as thou hast loved me. John 17:21–23

> Therefore we are buried with him by baptism into death: that like as Christ was raised up from the dead by the glory of the Father, even so we also should walk in newness of life. For if we have been planted together in the likeness of his death, we shall be also in the likeness of his resurrection. Knowing this, that our old man is crucified with him, that the body of sin might be destroyed, that henceforth we should not serve sin. For he that is dead is freed from sin. Likewise reckon ye also yourselves to be dead indeed unto sin, but alive

unto God through Jesus Christ our Lord.
Rom. 6:4–7,11

For the law of the Spirit of life in Christ Jesus *has made me free from the law of sin and death.* Rom. 8:2

If we live in the Spirit, let us also walk in the Spirit. Gal. 5:25

And every man that has this hope in him purifies himself, even as he is pure. Whosoever abides in him sins not: whosoever sins has not seen him, neither known him. Little children, let no man deceive you: he that does righteousness is righteous, even as he is righteous. He that commits sin is of the devil; for the devil sins from the beginning. For this purpose the Son of God was manifested, that he might destroy the works of the devil. Whosoever is born of God does not commit sin; for his seed remains in him: and he cannot sin, because he is born of God. I John 3:3,6–9

Whereby are given unto us exceeding great and precious promises: that by these you might be partakers of the divine nature, having escaped the corruption that is in the world through lust.
II Peter 1:4

Many Christians are in consternation upon reading these scriptures. This has been a point of confusion for many, because every Christian who has ever walked the face of the earth has found that he has not had total victory over sin. Many commentators say this means that you don't habitually continue in a sin, but show me one Christian who has not habitually continued in a sin. In order to keep from doing that, you must be in total victory. Others have said that it means you are continually growing in victory over sin in your life. That is true, because it is a progressive perfect tense, but it also has a completion.

Hebrews 11 discusses great victories by faith, but it also talks about some who didn't get those victories.

And these all, having obtained a good report through faith, received not the promise: God having provided some better thing for us, that they without us should not be made perfect. Heb. 11:39–40

The word "perfect" is confusing for many, so we will use "complete." They should not be completed, *they would not have all that God has provided* in the atonement *without us.* There were some things that they had faith for and believed for, but God would not allow them to experience them until those at the end of the age have come in.

This is very simple to comprehend when you understand life. Life is always growing. The Scripture tells us that we are not born of a corruptible seed but of an incorruptible seed by the Word of God. When we are born again, the life of Christ is birthed inside us as a seed that must grow. When a seed reaches its maturity, it produces a flower like that which originally produced the seed. At first that seed doesn't look at all like the flower, the flower here being a picture of Christ. As the life of Christ starts working and growing in us, our perceptions begin to change completely, and a different life on the inside begins to grow. That seed breaks through and sends down some roots, begins to grow up and manifest itself as a little stock, and the next thing you know here comes a little leaf. In time we begin to bear the fruit of the Spirit, which is another way of describing the character of Christ. When that character is fully formed, Christ will be fully formed in us, bringing us into the image of that original flower from which the seed came.

The church is not going to go back to the days of the apostles in the early church — that was seed. According to the Book of Acts, they only had a few miracles every couple of years. We don't want to go back and just have a little power of God, the gifts and the anointing of the Spirit, without character! In this hour we are to come into the fullness of fruit, the fullness of Christian character, understanding and right relationship worked out in our life. When we do, we will come into the dimension of perfection described in these scriptures, which are just samples of what the Word promises. That is the meaning of the Day of Atonement for the church. We cannot find that fullness until the Day of Atonement is upon us. There is a time element, and Trumpets announces that we are headed into that time element.

We are sealed by the Holy Spirit of promise until the day of redemption, so we have a measure of the fruit of the Spirit of Christ in us that is continuing to grow, especially in this period between Trumpets and Day of Atonement. It is a time of affliction and judgment and letting God deal with us in the sin areas of our life. Relationships are something that should be focussed on because in genuine relationships of love, commitment and integrity before God, we are going to find areas where we are encountered with unrighteousness and we must responsibly respond to those encounters by allowing God to deal with those things and change us.

There comes a point in time when this is complete. You and I may even progress to the point where we have fully appropriated in our faith that which God has provided, but we cannot possess it in our experience until the time is right. According to Galatians, Abraham believed that Christ would come and pay the atonement. The Scripture says that God preached the gospel to Abraham through Isaac when he received him back from the dead. Nevertheless, although Abraham saw and believed the message of the gospel, he could not experience the miracle of the new birth because Christ was not yet crucified. **He had it in spirit but could not have it in manifestation until the time element was right.** There are things right now which we can believe for and possess in spirit but cannot have in manifestation until the time is right.

The Day of Atonement is when we so completely appropriate Calvary and have so fully put on the righteousness of Christ in our life that death will no longer have a claim on us. Death only has a claim on us because of sin. Because we have not fully appropriated Calvary, which is a full appropriation for the consequence of sin, we still suffer death. But the end–time church which is alive at the coming of the Lord will not suffer death but will be caught up together with those who were dead in Christ coming out of the grave to meet the Lord in the air. This company of people will not go through the grave because they have so fully appropriated Calvary that death no longer has a claim on them. As the Scripture says, the last enemy to be conquered is death. The Rapture is a great victory over the consequence of sin!

The Scripture says that Christ, after Passover, Unleavened Bread and Firstfruits, appeared to over 500 brethren at once before He ascended to the Father. It says in Acts 2 that there were about 120 in the upper room when the outpouring of the Holy Spirit took place. My question is, where were the other 380 evangelicals? They were brethren, they were disciples of

Christ, they saw the resurrected Christ in the flesh, but because of certain basic things in their character they were not in the upper room and they missed it! Jesus said the Rapture of the church will be as a thief in the night. You need to watch and pray and be ready. The Rapture could very easily be immediately after the Day of Atonement, but there will be those who are as sleepy Christians who have not trimmed their lamps, who don't have a burning flame, who don't have their character worked out. When that full appropriation opportunity comes, they could miss it and have to go on through the Tribulation.

If you are in a place of total commitment before God and are allowing Him to deal with your character, then at the point that the Day of Atonement comes you will receive all that God has. When you study the Word and the Holy Spirit shows you something in your life that does not measure up to His will, how do you respond? Do you pretend that it didn't happen? Do you acknowledge it or do you excuse it by saying that no one is perfect? Or do you say, "Lord, forgive me, I want to change, I want to overcome this problem. Deal with my life so that I might outgrow this and overcome." The one response is what God is looking for, the other has consequences that are negative to our life.

This completion will be is experientially new to the church because she has never kept this feast, although it isn't something that has never been in the Word. It has always been there, but this is the hour in which the church is coming to keep it. What would it have been like if you were in Israel in the day that Jesus was born? You were following the law, you were a Pharisee of the Pharisees, you were doing all that God ordained for your time. But now here comes John the Baptist saying, "Repent, for the kingdom of heaven is at hand." One day he announces, "Behold, the Lamb of God who takes away the sins of the world." Here is the one who is the fulfillment of all of these rituals and He is the one who is going to make the final atonement for us. If all of your life you thought in a particular pattern and followed what was right up to that point, this is going to come to you as something new and you will question it.

That is what Jesus' generation did when He came. Why would we be so presumptuous as to think that when He comes again, we, being of the same flesh and blood that the Israelis were made of, would be so much different?

We have the written Word that Jesus gave us. We have the Word that He relied upon. We have the Word for our final judgment of all these things. Jesus came and fulfilled 334 prophecies. To fulfill ten of them in a row would have a probability of one in ten billion. He said, "Search the scriptures, they witness of me. You would not come to me that you might have life." Isaiah the prophet says that the Word of God will not return to Him void but will accomplish that for which He sent it, but Jesus spoke to the Pharisees and said, "By your traditions you have made the Word of God of none effect."

What have the traditions of the church been that have made the Word of God of none effect? One obvious example is, "The day of miracles is past, it was all in the time of Jesus and the apostles." There has never been a day of miracles, only a God of miracles. Jesus is the same yesterday, today and forever. That cannot be changed. People have needed more in God to see miracles, so they say there aren't any.

You have to get back to the Book. What did Trumpets represent but the day of the open book? The book was brought out with special teaching and special illumination. There is new illumination needed to go on to the new feast, just as when Christ came it was the day of the open book in order to bring new understanding to the fulfillment of all that had gone before. So it is when Jesus returns and fulfills the prophecies surrounding the Second Coming of Christ. Our eyes must be enlightened, we must lift up our eyes to greater horizons, we must believe the Word of the Book. It was an amazing thing to them to believe the simple things of the Gospel of Jesus Christ, just as it is amazing to you and me to believe that there is such a full appropriation of Calvary that you can walk in victory over sin and that it will, in this generation, bring you to the great victory of the Rapture!

The church is being called on to keep the Day of Atonement. It isn't yet manifest, but it is a calling. No one had seen Jesus when John the Baptist began to preach that the kingdom of heaven was at hand, but it was a time of preparation. The period of Israel's visitation lasted three and-a-half years and then it ended.

Today, we are living in a time when we are seeing more Bible prophecy fulfilled than at any time since the incarnation of Jesus Christ. Every one of them is given signally in the Scripture as a sign of the times. I am sharing these things with you so that you might understand what they mean, that you might be prepared, and that you might receive what God has in this hour. It's the most fantastic day in which any person could ever live.

Father, open our hearts to see the significance of these days and make us responsive to the convicting work of the Holy Spirit in our lives so that we will be prepared to keep the Day of Atonement that is soon to be upon us. Amen.

THE DAY OF ATONEMENT PART II

We have seen that a seed planted in the ground doesn't bear a great resemblance to the flower that produced the seed, but as that seed grows and comes to maturity, it comes into the same image as that of the flower. The Day of Atonement speaks of *the full reproduction of that seed which is the life of Christ.*

I would like to now look at some of the things the Scripture says are means by which we are to come into this maturation and fulfillment. I first need to point out that there is no way biblically that we can look to the Rapture as a *means* of attaining the fulfillment of all that God has promised for our life. It must come by being worked out in our life here. Yes, we're saved, but our rewards and our placement in eternity are all dependent upon what happens in the growth and development of our character. The Church of Jesus Christ is to come to a completion (except for the body) before being raptured.

> And he gave some, apostles; and some, prophets; and some, evangelists; and some, pastors and teachers, for the perfecting of the saints, for the work of the ministry, for the edifying of the body of Christ: Till we all come in the unity of the faith, and of the knowledge of the Son of God, unto a perfect man, unto the measure of the stature of the fullness of Christ.
> Eph. 4:11–13

> But speaking the truth in love, may grow up into him in all things, which is the head, even Christ: From whom the whole body fitly joined together and compacted by that which every joint supplies, according to the effectual working in the measure of every part, makes increase of the body unto the edifying of itself in love. Eph. 4:15–16

There is a ministry provision by which the Body of Christ is to grow and mature until we come into the likeness and image of Christ, at which time these ministries will cease and we go home. These ministries are major provisions of God for us to grow into maturity. If we want to grow into the fullness that God has for us as individuals, we must recognize that it cannot be done outside of the context of the church and the ascension gift ministries that God has placed in the church.

131

In spite of any weaknesses that we might find in different believers or different bodies of believers, the Scripture shows us that we cannot come into fullness without partaking of these particular ministry provisions. Therefore, very early in our Christian walk we should settle in our own spirit our commitment to the Body of Christ and to the ministry gifts that God has placed in the Body, to see them continue to grow and mature that we might receive what God has for us. Anything that is less than responsible commitment is an enemy to this process and must be dealt with in our hearts by God's Word and Spirit so that we can go on to maturity and fullness.

> For when for the time you ought to be teachers, you have need that one teach you again which be the first principles of the oracles of God; and are become such as have need of milk, and not of strong meat. For every one that uses milk is unskillful in the word of righteousness: for he is a babe. Heb . 5:12,13

This is a biblical description of carnal Christians. They were old enough chronologically to be teachers, but they couldn't yet eat strong meat. They still had to have milk because they were unskillful in the word of righteousness — they didn't know God's Word effectively and by divine illumination.

> But strong meat belongs to them that are of full age, even those who by reason of use have their senses exercised to discern both good and evil. Heb. 5:14

Here we see that another aspect of growing into fullness and maturity is related to Christian service. If we are not involved in being part of the solution, then we will remain in the category of spiritual childhood. If we are not involved in being part of the ministry expression of the Body of Christ in one placement or another, the Scripture here teaches us that we are unskillful in the word of righteousness and have need of milk. **The one who comes into spiritual maturity does so by reason of use.** He has exercised his spiritual senses to discern both good and evil by reason of use.

> And these all, having obtained a good report through faith, received not the promise: God having provided some better thing for us, that they without us should not be made perfect. Heb. 11:39–40

This passage also tells us about relationship in the Body. The last generation of the church can expect to come into completion, but it will not get there alone. You cannot go into fullness all by yourself. We must gather as many as we can to bring them on with us. Joshua and Caleb were ready to enter the Promised Land and believed God for it, but they were not allowed to enter until the rest of the body was ready to go with them. We learn here that **the Day of Atonement is a time of commitment to the Body for maturation, character development and relationship with transparency and integrity.** The Body is to minister unto itself to increase in edification until we come into the likeness and image of Christ.

> Wherefore laying aside all malice, and all guile, and hypocrisies, and envies, and all evil speakings, as newborn babes, desire the sincere milk of the word, that you may grow thereby: If so be ye have tasted that the Lord is gracious. To whom coming, as unto a living stone, disallowed indeed of men, but chosen of God, and precious. Ye also, as lively stones, are built up a spiritual house, a holy priesthood, to offer up spiritual sacrifices, acceptable to God by Jesus Christ. Wherefore also it is contained in the scripture, Behold, I lay in Sion a chief corner stone, elect, precious: and he that believes on him shall not be confounded. Unto you therefore which believe he is precious: but unto them which be disobedient, the stone which the builders disallowed, the same is made the head of the corner. And a stone of stumbling, and a rock of offense, even to them which stumble at the word, being disobedient: whereunto also they were appointed. But you are a chosen generation, a royal priesthood, a holy nation, a peculiar [set apart] people that you should show forth the praises of him who has called you out of darkness into his marvelous light.
> I Peter 2:1–9

We are called together, we are to grow into this by the ministry of the Word.

> And I, brethren, could not speak unto you as unto spiritual, but as unto carnal, even as unto babes in Christ. I have fed you with milk, and not with meat: for hitherto you were not able to bear it, neither yet now

are ye able. For you are yet carnal: for whereas there is among you envying, and strife, and divisions, are you not carnal, and walk as men? I Cor. 3:1-3

The hindrance to growth is carnality that is divisionary, full of envying, strife, competition, etc. If these problems are in our life, they will hinder us from receiving strong meat. There is spiritual truth that God will not give to us as long as we allow these kinds of problems to exist in our life.

WE LEARN HERE ABOUT MEANS FOR ATTAINING WHAT IS IN THE DAY OF ATONEMENT. WE HAVE THE FIVE ASCENSION GIFT MINISTRIES THAT TEACH US THE WORD AND WHICH MINISTER TO US IN THE SPIRIT, TO EQUIP US SO THAT WE CAN GROW IN THE KNOWLEDGE OF GOD AND INTO HIS LIKENESS AND BE MORE EFFECTIVE IN OUR EXPRESSION OF MINISTRY. WE ARE TO GET INTO SERVICE AND BY REASON OF USE WE HAVE GROWTH, WHEREBY WE RECEIVE STRONG MEAT. AT THE SAME TIME, WE HAVE A COMMITMENT TO THE BODY TO SEE IT GROW AND IF WE HAVE ENVYING, STRIFE AND DIVISIONS (THE OPPOSITE OF COMMITMENT), THEN WE FIND IT HINDERS US FROM HAVING STRONG MEAT AND KEEPS US AS BABES NEEDING MILK. THEREFORE, GROWING INTO THE FULLNESS OF GOD AS HE INTENDS REQUIRES THESE KINDS OF COMMITMENTS.

All of the sacrifices, the feasts and the sabbath days were fulfilled and in their meaning with the one sacrifice of Jesus Christ, yet the believer has never entered in to all that was provided. We see this to be true by reading Hebrews 10:

For the law having a shadow of good things to come, and not the very image of the things, can never with those sacrifices which they offered year by year continually make the comers thereunto perfect. For then would they not have ceased to be offered? Because that the worshippers once purged should have had no more conscience of sins. But in those sacrifices there is a remembrance again made of sins every year. For it is not possible that the blood of bulls and of goats should take away sins. Wherefore when he comes into the world, he saith, Sacrifice and offering thou wouldest not, but a body hast thou prepared me: In burnt offerings and sacrifices for sin thou hast no pleasure. Then said I, Lo I come (in the volume of the book it is written of me) to do thy will, O God. Above when he said, Sacrifice and offering and burnt offerings and offering for sin thou wouldest not, neither hadst pleasure therein; which are offered by the law; Then said he, Lo, I come to do thy will, O God. He takes away the first [the law], that he may establish the second. By the which will we are sanctified through the offering of the body of Jesus Christ once for all. Heb. 10:1–10

THERE IS TO BE A TOTAL CLEANSING AND VICTORY OVER SIN BECAUSE OF CALVARY. *If it is not total because of Calvary, then Jesus has to come and die again because that's what the lambs and the bullocks did in the Old Testament.* They had that offering once a year on the Day of Atonement and for a year Israel was cleansed, and they had to go through it year after year. But if Christ's atonement is complete, it needed to only take place once. **The church has never experienced this fullness of victory over sin because the season has not been right.**

We have seen that on the Day of Atonement the high priest made an atonement for himself and an atonement for his house, and then he made an atonement for Israel. Christ made no atonement for Himself because He was without sin.

For every high priest taken from among men is ordained for men in things pertaining to God, that he may offer both gifts and sacrifices for sins: Who can have compassion on the ignorant, and on them that are out of the way; for that he himself also is compassed with infirmity. And by reason hereof he ought, as for the people, so also for himself, to offer for sins. And no man takes this honor unto himself, but he that is called of God, as was Aaron. So also Christ glorified not himself to be made a high priest; but he that said unto him, Thou art my Son, today have I begotten thee. As he saith also in another place, Thou art a priest forever after the order of Melchisedec. Heb. 5:1–6

Christ fulfilled this high priestly ministry. He came into the Day of Atonement in its fulfillment and offered a sacrifice for His house, which speaks of the church. The church of God is a reflection of the sanctuary in heaven. We need to understand that there was a cleansing of the heavenly realms that were defiled by the fall of Satan, but there is also to be a cleansing once and for all of the sanctuary, the church. Christ went within the veil and sprinkled His own blood for the cleansing of the church.

> But into the second went the high priest alone once every year, not without the blood, which he offered for himself, and for the errors of the people: The Holy Spirit this signifying, that the way into the holiest of all was not yet made manifest, while as the first tabernacle was yet standing: Which was a figure for the time then present, in which were offered both gifts and sacrifices, that could not make him that did the service perfect, as pertaining to the conscience.
> Heb. 9:7–9

This is in contrast to Christ's atonement that *can* make us perfect. The Holy Spirit was signifying here that the way into the Holiest of All was not manifest while the first tabernacle was standing. There are three applications. *First,* the Holiest of All is where God's manifest presence dwelt amongst His people. The way into that presence wasn't made manifest until Christ came. *Second,* the way to the heavenly presence in the throneroom of God was not manifest until Christ came. *Third,* as long as Adam, the old man, remains standing in our life and does not come under the cross, the way into the Holiest of All, the fullness of God, is not yet made manifest in us. Most of Israel worshipped God in the outer court, there were some who came in the priestly ministry and worshipped in the Holy Place, but in order to come into the Holy of Holies, the first tabernacle could not remain standing. When Adam is under the cross, the way into the Holiest of All, the presence of God, is made manifest. *There must be a full victory over Adam.*

> Having therefore, brethren, boldness to enter into the holiest by the blood of Jesus, by a new and living way, which he has consecrated for us, through the veil, that is to say, his flesh: And having a high priest over the house of God: Let us draw near with a true heart in full assurance of faith, having our hearts sprinkled from an evil conscience, and our bodies washed with pure water. Heb. 10:19–22

We have access into the presence of God by water and blood but have only realized this in a measure. Christ is the fore-runner within the veil for us that we might come into the fullness of His presence. We must recognize that there is a dimension of God's fullness that we have not yet experienced and that the Day of Atonement represents the *means of coming into the fullness of Christ* in God's time. The following scriptures are samples of what we are to come into.

> And he said, Men, brethren, and fathers, hearken; the God of glory appeared unto our father Abraham, when he was in Mesopotamia, before he dwelt in Charran. Acts 7:2

> And in the morning, then ye shall see the glory of the Lord; for that he hears your murmurings against the Lord: and what are we, that ye murmur against us? Exo. 16:7

These verses speak of God's glory being seen by Abraham and by Israel. God's glory is a mystery to many and hard to define. However, **the glory of God speaks of at least the manifestation of God's presence in His nature, His essential attributes and in His power.**

The glory of God was seen by Moses when he said, "If I please thee, let me see thy glory." God said that no man could see His glory but He would allow Moses to see the backward part, and the glory of God passed before him. Moses was with God and His glory shone so brightly on Moses' face that the children of Israel couldn't look upon him and asked him to put a veil over his face. The glory of God began to stay in the tabernacle which Moses created. No one could enter within the veil except on the Day of Atonement when the high priest entered in. God's glory in Christ when He came to dwell in human flesh. We read in Matthew 17 of the Mount of Transfiguration where Jesus was transfigured and the glory of God was manifested.

> And was transfigured before them: and his face did shine as the sun, and his raiment was white as the light. Matt. 17:2

As the glory of God was manifested, His face was as bright as the sun and His clothing, because of the brightness emanating from Him, was as the light. Acts 7:55 speaks of

Stephen's face shining with the glory of God when he was martyred.

AND THERE IS A GLORY OF GOD THAT IS TO COME UPON THE END-TIME CHURCH. There is a dimension of the Holy of Holies that we cannot see and experience and participate in until the church keeps the Day of Atonement.

> Arise, shine; for thy light is come, and the glory of the Lord is risen upon thee. For, behold, the darkness shall cover the earth, and gross darkness the people: but the Lord shall arise upon thee, and his glory shall be seen upon thee. And the Gentiles shall come to thy light, and kings to the brightness of thy rising. Lift up thine eyes round about, and see: all they gather themselves together, they come to thee: thy sons shall come from far, and thy daughters shall be nursed at thy side. Then thou shalt see, and flow together, and thine heart shall fear, and be enlarged; because the abundance of the sea shall be converted unto thee, the forces of the Gentiles shall come unto thee. Isa. 60:1-5

This is a prophecy of the greatest harvest of souls in the history of the world. The glory of God is to come upon the church, **a glory and a fullness of victory over sin that we will not appropriate until the Day of Atonement** as the prepared kingdom of the antichrist is laying at the gate ready to come into ascendency! At this point in time, THE GLORY OF GOD WILL BE MANIFESTED THROUGH HIS PEOPLE, THE CHURCH, AND MULTITUDES WILL BE SWEPT INTO THE KINGDOM.

We see a picture of the glory of God on the church in Revelation 12:

> And there appeared a great wonder in heaven; a woman clothed with the sun, and the moon under her feet, and upon her head a crown of twelve stars.
> Rev. 12:1

Clothed with the sun means the glory of God. Jesus' face shone as the sun when He was transfigured. It's the glory of God on the church. What does this mean to us?

> For I reckon that the sufferings of this present time are not worthy to be compared with the glory which shall be revealed *in us*. Rom. 8:18

Remember, the ten-day period between Trumpets and Atonement is a time of testing and trial. THE SUFFERINGS OF THIS PRESENT TIME ARE NOT WORTHY TO BE COMPARED TO THE GLORY OF GOD THAT SHALL BE REVEALED IN US!

> To whom God would make known what is the riches of
> the glory of this mystery among the Gentiles; which is
> *Christ in you*, the hope of glory. Col. 1:27

We're not talking about the seed that was planted at the new birth, but *the seed having grown to full maturity in the heart of the believer.* As we look at our High Priest going in to make the atonement and the veil was rent as a way was made for the believer to have access into God's presence, we recognize our having experienced this presence only in a measure. However, with the other prophecies seen in the Scripture, we recognize that *there is a time when the fullness of Christ will come within His people and the glory of God will rise upon them and be manifest through the church to a lost world.* PASSOVER IS WHERE WE HAVE THE ORIGINAL ACCESS BY THE BLOOD, THE DAY OF ATONEMENT IS THE COMPLETION.

There were two goats on the Day of Atonement, both of which had to be without spot or wrinkle. A lot was taken and the one chosen as the scapegoat would live, and the other, called the goat for Jehovah, would die. Hands were laid on the goat designated to die as a symbol of the sins of the people being transferred to the goats. The goat for Jehovah died to reconcile, and the blood was taken by the high priest into the Holy of Holies and sprinkled seven times on the mercy seat as a sin offering. After the blood was sprinkled, the live goat would be taken out in the wilderness and let go.

> For the bodies of those beasts, whose blood is brought
> into the sanctuary by the high priest for sin, are
> burned without the camp. Wherefore Jesus also, that
> he might sanctify the people with his own blood,
> suffered without the gate. Let us go forth therefore
> unto him without the camp, bearing his reproach.
> Heb. 13:11-13

The animal's body was burned outside the camp of the children of Israel. So Jesus was crucified outside of Jerusalem on Golgotha Hill — a reproach.

There are a couple of aspects of the work of Calvary that are pictured in this dual offering because by typology it was impossible to show it with one goat. The goat known as the "scapegoat" was left alive. After the blood of the slain goat was sprinkled, hands were laid on the live goat and it was taken into the wilderness and let go. This speaks first of Christ in His resurrection. The Scripture tells us that if we have been saved by His death, how much more shall we be saved by His life, which speaks of the resurrection side of reconciliation. He not only died to reconcile, but He also lives to reconcile. Forgiveness means to "bear" or to "carry away." The Hebrew word "azazel," translated "scapegoat," literally is the goat for departure and *signifies entire removal*. **The sins of Israel were symbolically placed on the scapegoat, which was then taken out of the camp and let go, symbolizing the removal of sin.** They were looking forward in typology to the work of Calvary, where they would find not only forgiveness of sin by the blood but the removal of sin from their life.

THE DAY OF ATONEMENT SPEAKS OF a time when we are to come into a place of **NOT ONLY FORGIVENESS BUT THE REMOVAL OF SIN, OR RIGHTEOUSNESS IMPLEMENTED IN THE LIFE OF THE BELIEVER.** We have seen every other feast, even through Trumpets, fulfilled with this kind of application to the church, which tells us that out of consistency the Day of Atonement must also have this application. Remember that the number 2 always points to Christ and His church as a testimony. The scapegoat was presented with the Lord's goat to Jehovah; so the church is to be presented before God with Christ. The scapegoat was to be without spot or blemish. As we read in Ephesians 5:26–27, the High Priest, the Lord Jesus Christ, washes us by the washing of the water of the Word that the church might be without spot, blemish or wrinkle or any such thing. We find that the scapegoat shared in the ministry of reconciliation because it was reconciling by life and the removal of sin.

The only people who have ever shared in the ministry of reconciliation are the people of God.

> Therefore if any man be in Christ, he is a new creature: old things are passed away; behold, all things are become new. And all things are of God, who has reconciled us to himself by Jesus Christ, and has

given to us the ministry of reconciliation.
II Cor. 5:17-18

We are Christ's ambassadors with a ministry of reconciliation. **THE SCAPEGOAT LIVED TO RECONCILE, WHILE THE LORD'S GOAT DIED TO RECONCILE. THE LORD DIED TO RECONCILE, BUT BECAUSE HE ROSE AGAIN, WE LIVE!** *The scapegoat has been spoken of* by some commentators *as representing the removal of Satan and the evil one.* Here we find the same parallel because Satan was defeated at Calvary and the scapegoat was used, as are Christ and the church, to subdue the evil one.

THE ATONEMENT INCLUDES A PERIOD OF DEVELOPING RIGHTEOUSNESS. IT INCLUDES A PURIFYING OF THE BELIEVER'S LIFE UNTIL WE COME INTO THE FULLNESS OF CHRIST THROUGH THE MINISTRY OF THE FIVE ASCENSION GIFT OFFICES, THROUGH THE MINISTRY OF THE WORD, THROUGH THE MINISTRY OF THE BODY AND THROUGH CHRISTIAN SERVICE. THERE IS ACCESS INTO THE GLORY OF GOD BUT NOT IN ITS COMPLETENESS UNTIL THE TIMING IS RIGHT, AND THERE IS A FULLER DIMENSION OF THE GLORY OF GOD THAT WILL BE SEEN AT COMPLETION. JESUS CHRIST WAS THE GLORY OF GOD MANIFESTED IN HUMAN FLESH, BUT ON THE DAY THAT HE WAS AT THE MOUNT OF TRANSFIGURATION, HE COMPLETED HIS JOURNEY AS THE SON OF MAN AND CAME DOWN FROM THE MOUNT, WENT STRAIGHT TO JERUSALEM AND WAS CRUCIFIED. AS THE CHURCH COMES TO ITS COMPLETION, IT ALSO WILL FIND THAT THE GLORY OF GOD WILL BE UNVEILED FOR WE ARE HIS WORKMANSHIP. HE WILL PULL ASIDE THE VEIL OF THE FLESH THAT THE GLORY MIGHT BE MANIFEST, JUST AS IT WAS WITH CHRIST ON THE MOUNT OF TRANSFIGURATION.

Finally, as we see this reconciliation brought to the church, we know that it is through the blood sprinkled seven times, seven being the number of perfection. Everything that we have in God is on the foundation of the blood, from the beginning at Passover to completion at the Day of Atonement.

Much more then, being now justified by his blood, we shall be saved from wrath through him. Rom. 5:9

We are justified before God by the blood of Jesus Christ, just as if we had never sinned.

The cup of blessing which we bless, is it not the communion of the blood of Christ? The bread which we break, is it not the communion of the body of Christ? I Cor. 10:16

The blood is the only reason we *have fellowship with God.*

In whom we have redemption through his blood, the forgiveness of sins, according to the riches of his grace. Eph. 1:7

If I was a multimillionaire and said, "You can have whatever you want according to my riches," giving you a check for $100,000 would not reflect my riches. To be reflective of my riches, I might have to give you ten million dollars. In Christ, *we have redemption through His blood according to the riches of His grace.*

But now in Christ Jesus ye who sometimes were far off are made near by the blood of Christ. Eph. 2:13

God is omnipresent; how can one be far off? When you are separated from Him, there is a gulf between you, your relationship is broken, there is no union. But he that is joined to the Lord is one Spirit. *Through the blood we have union, nearness and proximity with the Lord.*

In whom we have redemption through his blood, even the forgiveness of sins: And, having made peace through the blood of his cross, by him to reconcile all things unto himself; by him, I say, whether they be things in earth, or things in heaven. Col. 1:14,20

The world has looked all over for peace, but there is no peace for the wicked, the Scripture says. *There is peace in the blood of Jesus.*

And almost all things are by the law purged with blood; and without shedding of blood is no remission. Heb. 9:22 Of how much sorer punishment, suppose ye, shall he be thought worthy, who hath trodden under foot the Son of God, and hath counted *the blood of the covenant* wherewith he was sanctified, an unholy thing, and hath done despite unto the Spirit of grace? Heb. 10:29

We come into covenant relationship because of the blood. We do not understand what is meant by covenant here, because you and I live in a world that has little commitment to anything. However, everything that we have in God is in a covenant with Him, backed up by five immutables, things that are unchangeable. God's Word is settled forever and changes not; He has given His oath; there has been the blood of Jesus; the life of Christ has been deposited in our spirit; and there is the seal of the covenant with the Holy Spirit. These five immutables are given to assure us of His faithfulness to His covenant. By the blood covenant, we are predestined to be found in His likeness and image, to be co-rulers with Christ as the Bride of Christ, to be co-equals with Him and joint heirs of all that is Christ's.

> Now the God of peace that brought again from the dead our Lord Jesus, that great shepherd of the sheep, through the blood of the everlasting covenant.
> Heb. 13:20

Jesus Christ rose from the grave because of the blood covenant. The power of the blood is so powerful that it took dominion over death!

> How much more shall the blood of Christ, who through the eternal Spirit offered himself without spot to God, purge your conscience from dead works to serve the living God? Heb. 9:14

Only the blood of Jesus can remove guilt from your conscience. The American Medical Association tells us that over 80% of the sickness in our country can be attributed to unresolved guilt. Guilt cannot be removed by a psychologist's couch, hypnotism, EST, the power of positive thinking or positive confession. Only the blood of Jesus Christ can purge your conscience from guilt.

> For it is not possible that the blood of bulls and of goats should take away sins. Having therefore, brethren, boldness to enter into the holiest by the blood of Jesus. Heb. 10:4,19

We come into the presence of God only through the blood of Jesus Christ.

> But if we walk in the light, as he is in the light, we have fellowship one with another, and the blood of Jesus Christ his Son cleanses us from all sin.
> I John 1:7

The blood of Jesus is the only cleansing from sin.

> Whom God has set forth to be a propitiation through faith in his blood, to declare his righteousness for the

143

remission of sins that are past, through the forbearance of God. Rom. 3:25

Propitiation is a sacrifice offered to appease the wrath of God. *The blood of Jesus is the only thing that will appease the wrath of God* on your life as a sinner.

And they overcame him by the blood of the Lamb, and by the word of their testimony; and they loved not their lives unto the death. Rev. 12:11

One of the ways that *you can overcome the enemy is by the blood of Jesus Christ.*

If we are going to understand the meaning of the Day of Atonement, we must recognize right from the outset that CENTRAL TO THE WHOLE EVENT OF THE DAY WAS THE SHED BLOOD OF THE LAMB. SO IT IS THAT YOU AND I ARE GOING TO FIND THAT AS WE KEEP THE DAY OF ATONEMENT, WE WILL FIND A NEW DIMENSION AND A NEW POWER IN THE BLOOD, A NEW APPROPRIATION OF WHAT THE BLOOD HAS GIVEN US, AN UNDERSTANDING OF THE BLOOD COVENANT AND ITS POWER AND OF GOD'S COMMITMENT TO US. "No greater love has any man than this: that he lay down his life for his friends."

When I was taking a genetics class, I discovered that the blood in the human body basically comes from the male contribution to the fetus. Jesus had no earthly father. The blood that pumped through His veins was the product of God the Holy Spirit that came upon Mary when she was impregnated. The blood of Jesus Christ, therefore, was efficacious. The life is in the blood, the Scripture says. Stop and think about all that is meant by the blood of Christ that was shed for us. It not only brought reconciliation through death, but it brought life because it raised Him from the dead. The life is Spirit, and the life is in the blood; **the blood and the Spirit are one.**

THE DAY OF ATONEMENT WILL FIND ITS FULFILLMENT ONLY ON THE BASIS OF THE BLOOD COVENANT. I believe one of the things that we will learn about in this last hour, by the revelation of the Spirit, is a greater dimension of understanding of the effect and meaning of the blood. The central heartbeat of the Day of Atonement is centered around the work of the blood of the Lamb; this means that you and I should begin to have a new focus on the work of the blood in our lives to bring us on to fullness.

I pray that this helps you to find some practical direction in the understanding of this feast period and that you will pursue it with your heart to find character development, relationship in the Body, service, a hunger for the Word, an understanding of the gift ministries that God has put in the Body and what they mean for us, and an understanding of the blood. These are all practical areas that we can immediately apply to our life in order to grow and mature in Him.

Father, we thank you for your Word. We thank you for this wonderful series of pictures that you have given us through the feasts. We thank you for the enlightening commentary on these pictures in the New Testament. And, Father, as we would look towards these particular purposes of your Spirit in this hour, we're asking that you will help us to become related. Teach us about relationships, teach us what it means to be committed in the body to one another, teach us what it means to search your Word, to eat from your Word. Teach us what it means to enter into Christian service, finding an expression so that we can lay hold of strong meat and grow thereby. Teach us, Lord, what it means to break away from divisionary attitudes in our heart or envyings or strife of any kind. Teach us, Lord, to understand more deeply the work of the blood in order that through those foundations and through the wonderful blood covenant we might go on to completion. Amen.

THE FEAST OF BOOTHS

Speak unto the children of Israel, saying, The fifteenth day of this seventh month shall be the feast of tabernacles for seven days unto the Lord. Lev. 23:34

Also in the fifteenth day of the seventh month, when you have gathered in the fruit of the land, you shall keep a feast unto the Lord seven days: on the first day shall be a sabbath, and on the eighth day shall be a sabbath. And you shall take you on the first day the boughs of goodly trees, branches of palm trees, and the boughs of thick trees, and willows of the brook: and you shall rejoice before the Lord your God seven days. And you shall keep it a feast unto the Lord seven days in the year. It shall be a statute for ever in your generation: you shall celebrate it in the seventh month. You shall dwell in booths seven days: all that are Israelites born shall dwell in booths: That your generations may know that I made the children of Israel to dwell in booths, when I brought them out of the land of Egypt: I am the Lord your God. And Moses declared unto the children of Israel the feasts of the Lord. Lev. 23:39-44

For I will cast out the nations before thee, and enlarge thy borders: neither shall any man desire thy land, when thou shalt go up to appear before the Lord thy God thrice in the year. Exo. 34:24

The three times were the feast periods of Passover, Pentecost and Tabernacles. The first thing that we see pictured in *Tabernacles is a feast of unity* which took place the day following the Day of Atonement. All of Israel was to come in and participate in the feast. They were not to be afraid to come out of their land.

Think about this. Here you are in a city perhaps 150 miles away from Jerusalem and you are going there to keep the feast. You leave your plot of land and there is no one left to guard it, but God's promise is that no one will plunder it, He will not suffer the enemy to destroy it. **It is a picture not only of the unity of the entire body coming together, but also of a lack of fear to leave the fenced plot of sectarianism.** Sectarianism has to do with identifying denominationally with this or that group instead of with the entire Body of Christ.

This is the first aspect of the Feast of Tabernacles. Its parallel is the fulfillment of what Jesus prayed in John 17:

> That they all may be one; as thou, Father, art in me, and I in thee, that they also may be one in us: that the world may believe that thou hast sent me. And the glory which you gave me I have given them; that they may be one, even as we are one: I in them, and thou in me, that they may be made perfect in one; and that the world may know that thou hast sent me, and hast loved them, as thou hast loved me. John 17:21-23

The kind of oneness that Jesus had with the Father is a picture of the Body of Christ in unity with each other and in Him. The unity that Jesus had with the Father was such that He said, "The words that I speak unto you, I receive a commandment what I should say and what I should speak. I do nothing but what I see the Father do. Hitherto I work and the Father works, and the works that I do, it is not I that am doing them but the Father that dwells in me." Jesus prayed that the church would mature into this kind of unity. We must bear in mind that only after Passover, Unleavened Bread, Firstfruits, Pentecost, Trumpets and the Day of Atonement does this kind of unity come into realization.

> Now I beseech you, brethren, by the name of our Lord Jesus Christ, that you all speak the same thing, that there be no divisions among you; but that you be perfectly joined together in the same mind and in the same judgment. I Cor. 1:10

> For who has known the mind of the Lord, that he may instruct him? But we have the mind of Christ.
> I Cor. 2:16

> Till we all come in the unity of the faith, and of the knowledge of the Son of God, unto a perfect man, unto the measure of the stature of the fullness of Christ.
> Eph. 4:13

There are several areas by which you can identify a minister of the Lord. One of the best ways is to recognize that only God's sheep will know God's shepherds. If you do not know the voice of the Lord, you will not know the voice of His servant. However, if you know the voice of God, you will find that the voice of His servant is such that it is in many ways like an echo of what the Spirit of God has been saying to your life. Things that you may have been sensing in your spirit and have not been able to verbalize or bring into clear focus will be coming forth from His servants.

A proven ministry of the Lord will love the flock: "I am the good shepherd: the good shepherd gives his life for the sheep" (John 10:11).

I know both how to be abased, and I know how to abound. Phil. 4:12

If he is a true servant of the Lord, he will not be covetous, he will not seek his own at the expense of the Body of Christ.

He that speaks of himself seeks his own glory: but he that seeks his glory that sent him, the same is true, and no unrighteousness is in him. John 7:18

He will also be very willing to minister in small groups as well as in large ones, as the Lord would direct. Although Jesus would go out and minister to the multiplied thousands, He always had time for the individual.

You can also discern the servant of God by the fruit of the Spirit. Jesus said, "You shall know them by their fruit." The servant of the Lord will also be able to discern the Body of Christ. He who does not discern the Body of Christ and speak of, minister to and identify with the Body of Christ is showing a weakness as a true servant of God.

THE FIRST THING WE RECOGNIZE ABOUT TABERNACLES IS THAT IT IS TO BE A FEAST OF UNITY IN WHICH THE BODY OF CHRIST IS TO COME INTO ONENESS OF SPIRIT AND THAT THIS ONENESS WILL BE MANIFEST WITH THE SAME JUDGMENT, THE SAME MIND OR KNOWLEDGE OF THE FAITH AND THE THINGS OF GOD. In other words, their doctrinal foundations will be one. They will have a union with the Lord like unto the union the Lord had with the Father during the incarnation. The five ascension gift ministries and the ministry of the Word and of the Spirit, things which we saw under the Day of Atonement, are a part of the means which will bring this to pass. *When we find righteousness implemented, we have unity* — not something that is sought as a goal but *the byproduct of right relationship with our heavenly Father and with our fellow man.* It is an automatic result. The only place you can have genuine unity is in the

Spirit around truth. You cannot have genuine unity over a lie, because certainly you could have no union with God in a lie.

The next thing that we learn about *the Feast of Tabernacles is that it is to be a feast of joy.* The Israelis were to build booths and rejoice throughout the whole week, and that joy should be a part of this great feast period.

> And thou shalt rejoice in thy feast, thou, and thy son, and thy daughter, and thy manservant, and thy maidservant, and the Levite, the stranger, and the fatherless, and the widow, that are within thy gates. Deut. 16:14

The fruit of righteousness, the Scripture says, is peace. The Scripture says that the Kingdom of God is not in meat or drink but in righteousness, peace and joy in the Holy Spirit. Righteousness is obedience to the revealed Word of God; as you walk in the revealed Word of God, there is a fruit that comes in your life which is peace, and out of that peace comes joy.

Because the church is in the process of restoration, we find that the pattern of the feasts is the exact pattern of truth that God has been establishing in the church of Jesus Christ coming out of religious captivity. This is parallelled with Israel's captivity in Babylon.

> By the rivers of Babylon, there we sat down, yea, we wept, when we remembered Zion. We hanged our harps upon the willows in the midst thereof. For there they that carried us away captive required of us a song; and they that wasted us required of us mirth, saying, Sing us one of the songs of Zion. How shall we sing the Lord's song in a strange land? Ps. 137:1-4

There is a song of the Lord that is not in the hearts of God's people when they are in captivity. The Scripture likens the believer unto an eagle, which is one of the most majestic birds in the world. That bird will soar high in the sky, it has an eye that can perceive miles away with great accuracy. It rides upon the currents and hardly has to flap its wings. But when you bring an eagle into captivity, it becomes one of the dirtiest of all birds. In captivity there is no song, there is no joy. When we do not keep obedience to the will of God, we come into captivity.

> The field is wasted, the land mourns; for the corn is wasted: the new wine is dried up, the oil languishes. Be ye ashamed, O ye husbandmen; howl, O ye vinedressers, for the wheat and for the barley; *because the harvest of the field is perished.* The vine is dried up, and the fig tree languishes; the pomegranate trees, the palm tree also, and the apple tree, even all the trees of the field, are withered: *because joy is withered away from the sons of men.* Joel 1:10–12

When we don't keep Tabernacles and don't have that joy, a harvest is lost.

> The elders of the daughter of Zion sit upon the ground, and keep silence: they have cast up dust upon their heads; they have girded themselves with sackcloth: the virgins of Jerusalem hang down their heads to the ground. Mine eyes do fail with tears, my bowels are troubled, my liver is poured upon the earth, for the destruction of the daughter of my people; because the children and the sucklings swoon in the streets of the city. They say to their mothers, Where is corn and wine? when they swooned as the wounded in the streets of the city, when their soul was poured out into their mothers' bosom. Lam. 2:10–12

WHERE IS THE CORN AND THE WINE? The corn and the wine are symbols of fruit, of maturity: the fruit of souls and the fruit of the Spirit. They might have been asking the church of Jesus Christ, Where is your victory over sinful habits? Where is this holiness of life? Where is the mind of Christ that you are to have? Where is the power of the Spirit? Where is your freedom from bitterness and malice? Where is your desire to intercede and really pour out your life to a lost world? It is as an accusation from the world to the church when the harvest is perished and when the joy has withered from the people.

However, one of the signals of Tabernacles being kept is to be joy. Jeremiah 33:11 speaks of the restoration of Israel coming out of Babylon. They would have the voice of the bride and of the bridegroom; they would come in with a sacrifice of praise to the Lord; there would be joy and dancing and rejoicing. This has its parallel application to the church coming out of religious Babylon. Religious Babylon is where the church fell during the Dark Ages into liturgy, forms, rituals, a system of works, a pattern of religion without the reality of the presence of God often substituting formula and method for relationship with Him. Isaiah prophesied of the period of restoration in Tabernacles:

> But be ye glad and rejoice for ever in that which I create: for, behold, I create Jerusalem a rejoicing, and her people a joy. And I will rejoice in Jerusalem, and joy in my people: and the voice of weeping shall be no more heard in her, nor the voice of crying.
> Isa. 65:18–19

Many believers sing in the Spirit with gusto now, but we haven't seen anything of the sense of joy that the Feast of Tabernacles really represents. In contrast to the time of downsitting when Israel went into Babylonian captivity, we read in Psalm 126 of when they came out:

> When the Lord turned again the captivity of Zion, we were like them that dream. Then was our mouth filled with laughter, and our tongue with singing: then said they among the heathen, The Lord hath done great things for them. The Lord hath done great things for us; whereof we are glad. Ps. 126:1–3

Have you ever listened to the world's music? "Ohhh, nobody loves me. Where were you when I needed you? I'm a loser. Poor me. You ran off with somebody else, but I can't stop loving you." The whole world buys it! But that is not the voice of the church in the last day. The voice of the church is one of rejoicing, of laughter and of joy and of singing! IN KEEPING THE FEAST OF TABERNACLES, THE CHURCH IS GOING TO BE CHARACTERIZED BY A SENSE OF JOY THAT THE WORLD DOES NOT KNOW, A REJOICING, A LAUGHTER, AN EXCITEMENT, A LIGHTNESS, A FULLNESS, A HAPPINESS, THAT CANNOT BE KNOWN IN THE WORLD.

Babylon means confusion, and those who make friends with the worldly system are in confusion. James 4:4 says, "Ye adulterers and adulteresses, know ye not that the friendship of the world is enmity with God? Whosoever therefore will be a friend of the world is the enemy of God." That does not mean that you aren't to love the lost, but it does mean that you are not to make friendship with the world system. There is no fellowship with light and darkness.

We next learn that it is *a feast of ingathering*, something to be brought in.

> And the feast of harvest, the firstfruits of thy labor, which thou hast sown in the field: and *the feast of ingathering*, which is in the end of the year, when thou hast gathered in thy labors out of the field. Exo. 23:16

This took place at the end of the *agricultural year.* Passover was at the beginning of the year, the first month on the calendar of Israel. The seventh month is the end of the agricultural year, then come the winter months. Prophecy also speaks of it as the first month in the *civil calendar.* THE SEVENTH MONTH OF THE AGRICULTURAL CALENDAR WAS THE FIRST MONTH OF THE CIVIL CALENDAR. This feast was at the end of the harvest, which speaks of the work of God at the end of the age.

> Jesus said, Do not gather them up lest while you gather up the tares, ye root up also the wheat with them. Let them both grow together until the harvest: and in the time of harvest I will say to the reapers, *Gather ye together first the tares,* and bind them in bundles to burn them: but *gather the wheat into my barn.* Matt. 13:29–30

> Then Jesus sent the multitude away, and went into the house: and his disciples came unto him, saying, Declare unto us the parable of the tares of the field. He answered and said unto them, He that soweth the good seed is the Son of man; The field is the world; the good seed are the children of the kingdom; but the tares are the children of the wicked one; The enemy that sowed them is the devil; the harvest is the end of the world; and the reapers are the angels. As therefore the tares are gathered and burned in the fire; so shall it be in the end of this world. The Son of man shall send for his angels, and they shall gather out of his kingdom all things that offend, and them which do iniquity; And shall cast them into a furnace of fire: there shall be wailing and gnashing of teeth. Then shall the righteous shine forth as the sun in the kingdom of their Father. Who hath ears to hear, let him hear. Matt. 13:36–43

This parable speaks of a time at the **end of the age when the things that offend will be removed out of the believer's life (keeping the Day of Atonement) or removing those who do not allow righteousness to be implemented in their lives (the great apostasy). As a result of this activity, the righteous will show forth the glory of God, bringing in the greatest harvest of souls the world has ever seen.** There is to be a tremendous end–time harvest of the fruit of the Spirit and the fruit of souls, greater than any in history.

> For the Lord shall comfort Zion: he will comfort all her waste places; and he will make her wilderness like Eden, and her desert like the garden of the Lord; joy and gladness shall be found therein, thanksgiving, and the voice of melody. Isa. 51:3

> The wilderness and the solitary place shall be glad for them; and the desert shall rejoice, and blossom as the rose. It shall blossom abundantly, and rejoice even with joy and singing: the glory of Lebanon shall be given unto it, the excellency of Carmel and Sharon, they shall see the glory of the Lord, and the excellency of our God. Isa. 35:1–2

Song of Solomon speaks of two different experiences for the bride, a picture of the church:

> A garden enclosed is my sister, my spouse; a spring shut up, a fountain sealed. Song of Sol. 4:12

> Awake, O north wind; and come, thou south; blow upon my garden, that the spices thereof may flow out. Let my beloved come into his garden, and eat his pleasant fruits. Song of Sol. 4:16

In Bible typology the north wind speaks of adversity, the south wind of blessing. You need to go through the time of blessing, but there is also to be a time of adversity. What did Haggai say about Tabernacles?

> For thus saith the Lord of hosts; Yet once, it is a little while, and I will shake the heavens, and the earth, and the sea, and the dry land; And I will shake all nations, and the desire of all nations shall come: and I will fill this house with glory, saith the Lord of hosts. The

silver is mine, and the gold is mine, saith the Lord of hosts. The glory of this latter house shall be greater than of the former, saith the Lord of hosts: and in this place will I give peace, saith the Lord of hosts.
Hagg. 2:6-9

The shaking is a time of trial and adversity to remove the unclean things, followed by the manifestation of the glory of the Lord in the latter house. This manifestation of the glory is the blowing of the south wind.

For, lo, the winter is past, the rain is over and gone; The flowers appear on the earth; the time of the singing of birds is come, and the voice of the turtle is heard in our land. Song of Sol. 2:11-12

It is a time of fruit bearing, the ingathering. How do these scriptures relate in the New Testament?

Be patient therefore, brethren, unto the coming of the Lord. Behold, the husbandman waits for the precious fruit of the earth, and has long patience for it, until he receive the early and latter rain. James 5:7

There is a fruit of the earth to be received, and the Father waits for the early and the latter rain to bring the fruit to maturity that the harvest may be reaped. There is to be an outpouring of the Holy Spirit by which this is brought to pass. Joel has prophesied of these events:

Be glad then, ye children of Zion, and rejoice in the Lord your God: for he has given you the former rain moderately, and he will cause to come down for you the rain, the former rain, and the latter rain in the first month. And the floors shall be full of wheat, and the fats shall overflow with wine and oil. Joel 2:23-24

On the Day of Pentecost, Peter stood up during the outpouring of the Holy Spirit and said, "This is that which was spoken of by the prophet Joel." He was talking about the *former* rain, which is the Pentecostal experience. In the restoration of these truths to the church, we have seen the rain coming down in this century through the Baptism in the Holy Spirit and the gifts of the Spirit. The former rain is *moderate.* He said, *"I will give you the former rain and the latter rain in the first month,"* the first month of the civil year, the seventh month of the agricultural year — the former and latter rains at the same time.

Hosea prophesies, "I will come to you as the rain" and "He will come and rain righteousness upon you." Righteousness is to come upon us as rain. **There are these *pictures of the rain*: the outpouring of the Spirit, a coming of the Lord in a visitation of the Spirit of God; and a restoration of righteousness with the former and the latter rain. Righteousness and the outpouring of the Spirit come together for a purpose. The rain is poured out to water the seed of His life in us so that the fruit can come to maturity and be harvested. This is a picture of a visitation of God that brings to maturity. Without the rain there is no maturity. We are now in the former rain period.**

AT THE SECOND COMING OF CHRIST, HE IS NOT COMING TO LOOK FOR THE GIFTS OF THE SPIRIT IN YOUR LIFE. WHAT HE IS COMING FOR IS FRUIT. HE IS COMING AS THE LORD OF THE HARVEST, HE IS COMING AS THE HUSBANDMAN TO REAP THE HARVEST. The outpouring and visitation that we are just beginning to see in this present-day revival is something that will bring to maturation. Its purpose isn't just to have a bless-me club and say, "Oooh, that felt good." It's not to be slain in the Spirit. Fruit — that's the purpose of the visitation. Changed lives, transformed by the Spirit and by the Word.

Not only will this visitation of the Spirit bring fruit in the church, but it will bring the fruit of the spirit of antichrist. When light comes, you are held accountable. If you embrace light, it brings life; if you reject light, it brings condemnation. Wherefore, Jesus said in John 3:19, "This is the condemnation: that light came into the world and men loved darkness rather than light, and they would not come to the light lest they be reproved." That is what sends people to hell — not because they were born with a fallen nature, not because they were raised in a corrupt environment and got involved in sin. God forgives sin, but the reason people go to hell is because they reject the light of God that would set them free from sin. WHEN THIS OUTPOURING OF THE SPIRIT COMES TO THE CHURCH OF JESUS CHRIST AND IT GROWS IN THE LIGHT OF GOD, AND WHEN GOD'S LIGHT IS MANIFESTED AND THE WORD OF GOD IS PREACHED MORE FULLY, COMPLETELY AND EXTENSIVELY TO THIS WORLD, TWO THINGS ARE GOING TO HAPPEN. FIRST, THERE WILL BE THOSE WHO RECEIVE AND RESPOND TO

THIS OUTPOURING OF GOD'S SPIRIT AND RECEIVE LIFE. SECOND, THERE WILL BE THOSE WHO ARE PART OF THE KINGDOM OF ANTICHRIST WHO WILL REJECT THE LIGHT AND WILL MATURE IN DARKNESS — MATURING FOR JUDGMENT WHILE WE'RE MATURING TO GO HOME.

Tabernacles is to be a feast of rest. The children of Israel wandered in the wilderness for 40 years with some outstanding manifestations of the Spirit of God. They had seen God come visibly upon Mt. Sinai as fire by night and a cloud by day. He spoke to the entire nation audibly; they all heard Him speak the same thing. They saw the power of God in healing; every day they went out and gathered supernatural food that He supplied; they saw water come out of a rock to feed a whole nation. Yet Israel would not go into the land of promise when God gave them the opportunity. Ten of the spies were afraid and brought an evil report to Israel, who then failed to enter in because of unbelief in God's promise.

> And Joshua, the son of Nun, and Caleb the son of Jephunneh, which were of them that searched the land, rent their clothes: And they spake unto all the company of the children of Israel, saying, The land, which we passed through to search it, is an exceeding good land. If the Lord delight in us, then he will bring us into this land, and give it to us; a land which floweth with milk and honey. Only rebel not yet against the Lord, neither fear ye the people of the land; for they are bread for us: their defense is departed from them, and the Lord is with us: fear them not.
> Num. 14:6–9

But the congregation was full of unbelief and said they would not go in and possess the land. There are a few Joshuas and Calebs around now who have been inside and tasted a few things, have come back to tell the people about it and said, "Let's go."

IN THE ABOVE PASSAGE, ALL THEY HAD WAS A LITTLE FORETASTE OF THE PROMISED LAND. THE SCRIPTURE SAYS OF THE BAPTISM OF THE HOLY SPIRIT IN EPHESIANS 1:14 AND ROMANS 8:23 THAT THE CHURCH HAS AN EARNEST OF ITS INHERITANCE, JUST A LITTLE FORETASTE. The people of Israel went at the time of the first ripe grapes and had a wonderful momentary experience. What would it be like to live in Canaan, to drink there, to lay hold of the land and truly appropriate and live by the resurrection life of Jesus Christ? Not just for a moment to have the mind of Christ and a flash of a word of knowledge or a flash of prophecy or wisdom. Not for just a moment to have the gift of faith, not for a flash of God's power to break through that of the enemy. But to live there, abide there, walk in it day by day, moment by moment, *always* right there. That's the difference between the wilderness and the Promised Land. **A little taste of the things of the Spirit from time to time or abiding there. It's the difference between the Pentecostal experience and the Feast of Tabernacles to which we are headed.**

ISRAEL'S MISTAKE, DISOBEDIENCE WHEN GOD TOLD THEM TO GO IN AND TAKE THE LAND, IS THE CHURCH'S MISTAKE. God has given us a commandment and a promise and we are to go in. Israel was full of fear and unbelief; the church says, "Those things can't really happen" and it's full of fear of the giants in the land. Sure there are giants in the land, but if you walk with the Lord you drive the giants out!

THEY SEARCHED OUT THE LAND FOR 40 DAYS. THEY KNEW IT WAS A GOOD LAND WITH MILK AND HONEY; THEY KNEW GOD HAD TOLD THEM TO GO IN AND POSSESS IT, YET THEY REFUSED TO OBEY HIM AND CLAIMED THAT THEY DID NOT HAVE THE POWER OR THE AUTHORITY TO TAKE IT. I DON'T KNOW A BETTER PICTURE OF THE CHURCH THAN THIS. THE CHURCH HAD A FORETASTE AT THE RESTORATION OF PENTECOST BUT IT HAS FAILED TO GO IN AND POSSESS THE LAND. Many have returned to denominational ways instead of coming out of their fenced plots of sectarianism and identifying with the Body of Christ. They return to the same forms of ritualism that have no meaning and no life before God, including Pentecostal rituals. Others always talk about the move of God 40 years ago, but where is the move of God today? **Many are dying in the wilderness by trying to live on yesterday's victory.**

What was the wilderness experience really like? They had heavenly manna ("God gave me a new revelation of the Word and this scripture opened up"); water from the rock ("I was so thirsty but the Spirit of God moved on me and I feel so refreshed and lifted"); their clothes didn't wear out during those 40 years; God healed their sick and afflicted; they were protected from the enemy. *This is all that many Christians think there is.* They think, "If I can have God give me some fresh manna, if I can just get a little time of spiritual refreshing and blessing from the Lord, if my natural needs for shelter are taken care of, if I'm healed when I'm sick and the enemy can't give me a rout, then I know that I have all there is in this life before the Lord." BUT WHAT THEY HAVE DESCRIBED IS A WILDERNESS EXPERIENCE, AND THE SCRIPTURE SAYS THAT GOD DIDN'T BRING ISRAEL OUT OF EGYPT TO DIE IN THE WILDERNESS! HE BROUGHT THEM OUT IN ORDER THAT HE MIGHT TAKE THEM INTO THE PROMISED LAND, AND THAT IS EXACTLY WHAT HE WANTS TO DO WITH THE CHURCH. HE DIDN'T SAVE YOU, HE DIDN'T DELIVER YOU FROM DEMONIC POWERS AND POSSESSIONS AND HABITS, HE DIDN'T BREAK YOU FROM YOUR TIES TO THIS WORLD SO YOU COULD WANDER AROUND AS A HALF-BAKED PERSON AND DIE IN A WILDERNESS EXPERIENCE! HE BROUGHT YOU OUT SO YOU COULD BE CLEAN, BROKEN FROM THE WORLD AND BE ABLE TO GO INTO THE PROMISED LAND! IF YOU ARE SATISFIED WITH A WILDERNESS EXPERIENCE, YOU CAN'T HELP BUT BE A BIG DISAPPOINTMENT TO GOD. LET US FEAR, THE SCRIPTURE SAYS, LEST THE PROMISE BEING LEFT US OF ENTERING INTO HIS REST, ANY SHOULD SEEM TO COME SHORT OF IT. That's a healthy fear to motivate you in the right direction.

THE GENERATION THAT REFUSED TO TAKE THE LAND DIED IN THE WILDERNESS. There are Christians who are going to die in the wilderness. They will be in heaven, but they're going to miss much that was available for them, especially at the end of the age when these things are to be brought to fruition.

> All the commandments which I command thee this day shall ye observe to do, that ye may live and multiply, and go in and possess the land, which the Lord sware unto your fathers. And you shall remember all the way which the Lord thy God led thee these forty years in the wilderness, to humble thee, and to prove thee, to know what was in thine heart, whether thou would keep his commandments, or not. Deut. 8:1-2

The wilderness is a time of proving. It means you will be given options.

And he humbled you, and suffered you to hunger, and fed you with manna, which you knew not, neither did thy fathers know; that he might make thee know that man does not live by bread only, but by every word that proceeds out of the mouth of the Lord does man live. Deut. 8:3

As we prepare to go into the land of promise, God gives us a warning.

Beware that you forget not the Lord thy God, in not keeping his commandments, and his judgments, and his statutes, which I command you this day: Lest when you have eaten and are full and have built goodly houses, and dwell therein; and when your herds and your flocks multiply, and your silver and your gold is multiplied, and all that you have is multiplied; Then *thine heart be lifted up, and you forget the Lord your God, which brought thee forth out of the land of Egypt, from the house of bondage.*
Deut. 8:11-14

How shall I put thee among the children, and give thee a pleasant land, a goodly heritage of the hosts of nations? Jer. 3:19a

God, how can you grant that to us? **WHAT IS IT THAT YOU'RE LOOKING FOR IN OUR LIVES THAT WILL ALLOW YOU TO GIVE US OUR INHERITANCE IN ITS FULLNESS, NOT JUST A FORETASTE? WHAT ARE YOU LOOKING FOR?**

AND I SAID, THOU SHALT CALL ME, MY FATHER; AND SHALL NOT TURN AWAY FROM ME. Jer. 3:19b

He is interested in our love. So many Christians come to God as a vending machine: Lord, give me; thank you. Lord, give me; thank you. And all the time He has wanted us to say, "My father," and rejoice in our relationship with our heavenly Father and not turn away from Him. We look at Him as the head butler and the supply of our fun and games, and we forget about any relationship with Him. We value the blessing more than the one who gave it. How do you relate to others? "What can you mean for what I want in my life? How can you help me with what I want?" Is that how you relate to God? Every one of us has done it at one time or another, but the

Feast of Tabernacles pictures a time when we come to abide in the Spirit with a Christ-centered life.

> He that is entered into his rest, he also has ceased from his own works, as God did from his. Let us labor therefore to enter into that rest, lest any man fall after the same example of unbelief. Heb. 4:10-11

He has ceased from Adam and the self-life; he has learned what it means to abide in Christ and to continually abide in the Spirit. This is what coming into the land is and this is what Tabernacles is all about.

IN YOUR OWN SPIRIT YOU HAVE TWO CRIES: THE CRY OF ADAM THAT SAYS, "I DON'T HAVE THE POWER OR THE AUTHORITY, I CAN'T DO IT," AND THE CRY OF THE LIFE OF CHRIST PLANTED IN YOU AT THE NEW BIRTH SAYING, "YOU CAN DO ALL THINGS THROUGH CHRIST WHO STRENGTHENS YOU." RIGHT NOW, IN THIS DAY AND HOUR, THE SPIRIT OF GOD IS SPEAKING TO THE CHURCH OF JESUS CHRIST SAYING, "IT'S TIME TO PRESS IN. LET MY SPIRIT BE POURED OUT UPON YOU, LET THE OPEN REVELATION OF THE WORD WORK IN YOUR LIFE, EMBRACE THAT WHICH MY SERVANTS ARE SPEAKING TO YOU AND RECEIVE WHAT I'M DOING CIRCUMSTANTIALLY. LET THE WORD, THE SPIRIT, THE CIRCUMSTANCES AND THE MINISTRIES I'VE PLACED IN THE CHURCH WORK IN YOUR LIFE TO BUILD THE FRUIT, BECAUSE THE HOUR IS COMING WHEN YOU ARE TO GO IN AND TAKE THE LAND."

We're camped on the other side of the Jordan right now and are ready to cross over. The day before the Israelites crossed the river, Joshua said, "SANCTIFY YOURSELVES, FOR TOMORROW GOD WILL WORK WONDERS AMONG YOU, AND HEREBY YOU SHALL KNOW THAT THE LORD THY GOD IS WITH THEE: WITHOUT FAIL HE WILL DRIVE OUT BEFORE YOU YOUR ENEMIES." Everything that is in the way will be removed. The wheat will stand alone and be gathered home.

In each of our lives there is wheat and there are tares. In the natural, when the tare comes to maturity it stands straight up in the field; when the wheat comes to maturity it is always bent over carrying the weight. TRUE WHEAT IN THE BODY OF CHRIST CARRIES THE BURDEN OF THE SPIRIT IN THEIR HEART; THEY'RE BURDENED DOWN WITH WHAT

161

GOD WANTS TO DO FOR A LOST WORLD. THEY DON'T HAVE TO BE GOADED BECAUSE THEY HAVE AN INTRINSIC MOTIVATION IN THEIR HEART. INSTEAD OF BEING SELF-RIGHTEOUS AND PIOUS LIKE THE TARE, THE WHEAT IS HUMBLE ENOUGH TO ALLOW GOD TO DEAL WITH THEIR HEART. **As we come to keep the Day of Atonement and go on to Tabernacles, God is seeking to deal with and remove all the tares of our life so that we might be gathered home. The wheat is experiencing the removal of the tares from their heart; those who are tares respond to the dealings of God with self-justification and excuse, and because they won't allow God to take the tares out of their heart, they will be removed.**

Let's hear this and allow the Holy Spirit to deal with us and bring us into the land, removing the tares. Let's lay hold of the promise, let's press in to right priority of relationship with God and allow Him to bring us to right priority in relationship with one another. Let's hear what God is saying about where the church is to go and cooperate with the leading of the Holy Spirit that we might see His fullness.

Father, we thank you for your Word. We thank you for all that you're doing in this hour. We thank you, Father, that we have the privilege of living in a generation that will have the opportunity to go into the land. Father, help us not to miss the hour of our visitation. Lord, we recognize the developing process right now that we might be prepared at that moment and not be caught unawares, that we might be ready to take the land. Cause your Word to work in our heart, cause it to open our spirit that we would not be satisfied with a wilderness experience of a little fresh revelation, a little healing, a little refreshing of the Spirit, a little provision in the natural. Father, help us to go on to completion.

ON TO COMPLETION AND GOD'S GLORY

The convocation of tabernacles is the last of seven feasts outlined in the law of Moses, each one having a literal fulfillment in the Lord Jesus Christ, a prophetic fulfillment for the church, a fulfillment of an historical event in the history of Israel, and a personal application for our lives. We are currently between Trumpets and Atonement, which is why God is focusing on relationships, integrity and righteousness being implemented in our lives. Relationships that are full of commitment, integrity and transparency cause us to see weaknesses in our lives, areas that do not conform to the image of Christ. In that atmosphere we are finding that God requires that we allow His Spirit to change us where we need to be changed, and those who are not allowing that work of the Spirit to vitally take place in their lives are finding that they are without the vibrant manifest presence of God. We are now looking to completion during the Feast of Tabernacles, the final feast which ultimately leads to the physical return of the Lord and the setting up of the millennial reign.

We have seen that Tabernacles was a feast of unity, a feast of joy and rejoicing, a feast of ingathering — a great harvest of souls and fruit of the Spirit in Christian character — and a feast of rest where we learn to abide in Christ. We will have the capacity to abide in the manifest presence of God in the not-too-distant future. He usually gives us a foretaste of things to come, but we don't have enough spiritual capacity to abide there. As you grow in the Lord your spiritual capacity is enlarged and your ability to assimilate and incorporate those things are made a reality in your life, and pretty soon the truth which seemed so far off becomes a part of your everyday experience in God. You then go on from glory to glory, even into His likeness and image.

We need to keep this perspective in mind in the Christian walk. Many Christians have this kind of mentality: "I got saved, now I hang on, maybe God will bless me a little bit here and there, and when Jesus comes I get the great pie in the sky." I feel so sorry for them because they're missing so very, very much. The transformation process comes to completion for the generation that is alive at the coming of the Lord.

It comes to completion spiritually prior to Jesus' physical return, then follows the outer work physically when this mortality puts on immortality at the Rapture of the church and the coming of the Lord. We have seen the restoration process beginning as the church came out of the Dark Ages. We saw it beginning with Martin Luther and the truth of Passover being restored, followed by the Anabaptists and the truth of unleavened bread and firstfruits being restored; then the restoration of the Pentecostal Revival with the Baptism of the Holy Spirit; then the Charismatic Revival, the Feast of the Day of Trumpets, being established in the Body of Christ for the first time in the history of the church, a feast period that was also seeing its parallel with the covenant after the flesh with the regathering of Israel as a nation. The Yom Kippur War was a trumpet sound that we are to go on to Atonement. This pattern is perfect in history, in what God is doing in the church and in what God is doing in the world.

Redemption does have a definite completion. Jesus is the author and the finisher of faith, according to Hebrews 12. He begins faith and brings it to completion. The Christian experience, then, is one of growth from seed to maturity, which we have seen in Ephesians 4; the five ascension gift ministries are to function until we all come into the unity of the faith and of the knowledge of the Son of God unto a perfect man unto the measure of the stature of the fullness of Christ. That's completion! God is the Master Builder, He's not just haphazardly bouncing around with the church. We are the apple of His eye, the Body of Christ is the most important part of the creation on planet earth and, therefore, in the solar system, and everything else in this creation is minutely, meticulously in order and complete. God is not going to leave the church in a place of incomplete stature.

Paul's attitude about completion is shown in Philippians 3:

> Not as though I had already attained, either were already perfect: but I follow after, if that I may apprehend that for which also I am apprehended of Christ Jesus. Brethren, I count not myself to have apprehended: but this one thing I do, forgetting those things which are behind, and reaching forth unto those things which are before, I press toward the mark for the prize of the high calling of God in Christ Jesus. Let us therefore, as many as be perfect, be thus

minded: and if in any thing ye be otherwise minded, God shall reveal even this unto you. Phil. 3:12-15

This is the mental picture we should have. We're going somewhere, there is goal to be reached, there is a prize to be obtained.

But what things were gain to me, those I counted loss for Christ. Yea doubtless, and I count all things but loss for the excellency of the knowledge of Christ Jesus my Lord: for whom I have suffered the loss of all things, and do count them but dung, that I may win Christ. And be found in him, not having mine own righteousness, which is of the law, but that which is through the faith of Christ, the righteousness which is of God by faith: That I may know him, and the power of his resurrection, and the fellowship of his sufferings, being made conformable unto his death. Phil. 3:7-10

Many Christians' goal is to make the Rapture or to hang on to the end if they go by way of the grave. **The goal of Christian living is not an event in time, nor is it a place such as heaven.** We believe in heaven, but those aren't mansions that He is building for us. Understand the passage in John 14 to say that He is building a place in the Father's family with relationship and intimacy with your Creator. The placement that He has for you is not primarily physical. THE FULFILLMENT OF TABERNACLES, THE CONSUMMATION OF SALVATION, IS THE WINNING OF A PERSON. THE PRIZE THAT PAUL IS TALKING ABOUT IS JESUS. HE COUNTS ALL THINGS BUT LOSS THAT HE MIGHT WIN CHRIST!

To put it more specifically, the privilege of winning Christ and being a part of the Bride of Christ is the prize and a goal that is worthy of a lifetime of living. Not everyone is going to have the same thing in heaven. The thief who died on the cross next to Christ is saved, he is in heaven and he will forever be in the family of God, but he will never have the placement in the Father's family that the Apostles John, Paul and Peter have because he never QUALIFIED. Revelation 19 says that the Bride made herself ready and had arrayed herself with fine linen, clean and white, which is the righteous acts of the saints. CHRISTIAN CHARACTER, BEING FOUND IN THE LIKENESS AND IMAGE OF CHRIST, IS THE QUALIFIER. Paul said, "I have counted everything but loss,

I want to win Christ that I might know Him in the power of His resurrection that I might be found in His likeness, made conformable unto His death."

Some Christians even today have not attained that which is available to them. The things that we're talking about in Tabernacles will not be manifestly available until we go on through Day of Atonement. However, there are many things available now that were not in times past which people have not yet kept. All some people have is their fire insurance — the blood of the Lamb is applied but they haven't gone through water baptism, they have not kept Unleavened Bread and Firstfruits. Others have done all of this but they do not have the Baptism of the Holy Spirit. Others have not gone on to appropriate the Feast of Trumpets, they have not yet come out of their tribes and identified with the Body of Christ; they have not gone on to the call to war, they have not gone on to the call to keep the other feasts, and they're camped somewhere along the way. They're all Christians, they're all saved, but I Corinthians 15 says, "As one star differs from another in glory, so is the first resurrection."

There is something to be won, there is a completion to be attained. That is what this fulfillment of Tabernacles is all about, coming on to win the Person of Christ in His fullness. We all have Christ, you might say. That's true; we all have Christ in a measure, we all have authority over the power of the devil. But it is equally true that some people have more of Christ in their life than others; some have more of the anointing and blessing of God in their life than others; and some have more of the authority of the Spirit in their life than others. Not that any one individual has necessarily been given a certain special respect before God, because God is not a respecter of persons, but it is available to all. Paul prayed for the Galatian church, "I travail of you once again until Christ be *fully* formed in you." Between the initial partial formation and the full formation, there are many levels of differentiation, BUT WE ARE ALL CALLED TO KEEP THE FEAST OF TABERNACLES AND TO GO ON TO COMPLETION.

The Feast of Tabernacles was also a *feast of glory.* THE FULLNESS OF THE GLORY OF GOD IS TO BE RELEASED TO THE CHURCH DURING THE TIME THAT IT KEEPS THE FEAST OF TABERNACLES. Are you hungry for His glory? When I see just a little bit of His glory, I get so hungry and I say, "God, I can't stand as much as I see, but I want more!"

In Moses' wilderness tabernacle, the glory of God came in the midst of His people of Israel, dwelling in the Holy of Holies. No one had access to it but the high priest on the Day of Atonement. The ark was lost to the Philistines and was returned under David's Tabernacle, a picture of the last generation before the coming of Christ, which generation we are in. David's Tabernacle under the law showed the glory of God in the ark on Mount Zion where everyone had access to the manifest presence of God. Here there was a new dimension of worship, praise and communion with God that had never been available before, and which was not even available at Moses' Tabernacle where they still worshipped with liturgical forms.

We now come to Solomon's Temple which pictures Tabernacles:

> And all the men of Israel assembled themselves unto king Solomon at the feast in the month Ethanim, which is the seventh month. And all the elders of Israel came, and the priests took up the ark. And they brought up the ark of the Lord, and the tabernacle of the congregation, and all the holy vessels that were in the tabernacle, even those did the priests and the Levites bring up. And king Solomon, and all the congregation of Israel, that were assembled unto him, were with him before the ark, sacrificing sheep and oxen, that could not be told nor numbered for multitude. And the priests brought in the ark of the covenant of the Lord unto his place, into the oracle of the house, to the most holy place, even under the wings of the cherubims. I Kings 8:2-6

> And they drew out the staves of the ark, that the ends of the staves were seen from the ark before the oracle; but they were not seen without. And there it is unto this day. II Chron. 5:9

The ark had the staves removed, which meant it entered into rest and completion. The ark is a type of the manifest presence of God, and the temple is the church of Jesus Christ.

> It came even to pass, as the trumpeters and the singers were as one, to make one sound to be heard in praising and thanking the Lord; and when they lifted up their voice with the trumpets and cymbals and

instruments of music, and praised the Lord, saying,
For he is good; for his mercy endures forever: that
then the house was filled with a cloud, even the house
of the Lord; so that the priests could not stand to
minister by reason of the cloud: for the glory of the
Lord had filled the house of God. II Chron. 5:13-14

Notice what happened. The glory of God had been in Moses'
Tabernacle in a measure. Picturing the end of the church age,
ANYONE COULD COME BEFORE THE MANIFEST PRESENCE
OF GOD IN DAVID'S TABERNACLE IN A NEW DIMENSION OF
WORSHIP, LIBERTY, PRAISE AND COMMUNION WITH GOD.
In the very next generation, Solomon took the materials that
David had already purchased and the plan that David had
made, built the house of God and placed in it the ark of the
covenant. WHEN THEY DEDICATED THE TEMPLE, THE
GLORY OF GOD WAS SO GREAT AND SO POWERFUL THAT
NO MAN COULD STAND TO MINISTER!

AFTER THE ATONEMENT WE WILL SEE THE RETURN OF
THE GLORY OF GOD TO THE CHURCH IN ITS FULLNESS, A
FULLNESS THAT IT HAS NEVER KNOWN BECAUSE THE
CHURCH HAS NEVER BEFORE BEEN BROUGHT TO
COMPLETION. It was birthed with the glory of God, but not in
the measure of God's glory in the latter house. When a child is
born, there is much joy and excitement in the glory of the life
in that newborn child. When he comes to maturity, there is a
fullness of life about that child, assuming of course he was
raised in the nurture and admonition of the Lord. There is a
fullness in the intellectual capacity, in the emotional,
spiritual, physical and volitional capacities, the personality,
the talents, the abilities, the training, the expressions that
come through that person, all of which are phenomenal. The
glory is greater at the end than at the beginning, and so it is
with the church.

Something happened a few years later which pictures what
the antichrist will be doing in the world at the same time that
Tabernacles comes to fulfillment. The kingdom of Israel was
split in two between Solomon's two sons, Rehoboam and
Jeroboam, the latter not really serving God.

Whereupon the king took counsel, and made two
calves of gold, and said unto them, It is too much for
you to go up to Jerusalem: behold thy gods, O Israel,

which brought thee up out of the land of Egypt.
I Kings 12:28

Instead of keeping the feast in Jerusalem, which was under his brother's reign, he made false gods and made a *substitute feast.*

> And Jeroboam ordained a feast in the eighth month, on the fifteenth day of the month, like unto the feast that is in Judah, and he offered upon the altar. So did he in Bethel, sacrificing unto the calves that he had made: and he placed in Bethel the priests of the high places which he had made. So he offered upon the altar which he had made in Bethel the fifteenth day of the eighth month, even in the month which he had devised of his own heart; and ordained a feast unto the children of Israel: and he offered upon the altar, and burnt incense. I Kings 12:32-33

He built a substitute feast, and that is what the antichrist is doing in the world today. At the time that we come into the period of the Day of Atonement, we will find the true church of Jesus Christ going on and keeping the Feast of Tabernacles, while the devil will have a false feast and a false church.

> This know also, that in the last days perilous times shall come. For men shall be lovers of their own selves, covetous, boasters, proud, blasphemers, disobedient to parents, unthankful, unholy, without natural affection, trucebreakers, false accusers, incontinent, fierce, despisers of those that are good, traitors, heady, highminded, lovers of pleasures more than lovers of God; *Having a form of godliness, but denying the power thereof:* from such turn away. II Tim. 3:1-5

One of the definitions of "form" in the Webster's Dictionary reads "imitation of the image" — naming the name of Christ, having all the things that they say are Christian, yet without having Christ. I preached an entire message on that once in Southern California in 1969. Present there was a fellow who had been the winner of the world surfing championship that year who had just come from San Francisco, where he had been involved in a cult called the Brotherhood of Man. He thought he was really of God, but all he had was an imitation and he denied the power of God. People were being prayed for with the laying on of hands, going down under the power of

God, filled with the Holy Spirit, healed, the word of knowledge was being manifest, and this man would deny it all. Finally, in a special early service I spoke directly to him about the imitation of the image, of false brotherhood, the brotherhood of man instead of the brotherhood of the Spirit. That came through, and he got saved.

We have not seen anything yet about the falsity that is going to come in the name of Christ. You don't have to worry about getting caught up in the falsity as long as you have made Jesus Lord and are following His Word and the patterns of safety that God has given in the Scripture. There are several things involved in the patterns of safety: proven ministry; confirming it out of the mouths of two or three witnesses; it doesn't violate anything in the Scripture; biblical interpretation based upon the laws that are true for history, literature or law; finding your covering in right relationship in the local church; being rightly related to God and letting Him deal with your sin. If you are living right, you will be able to discern the voice of God's servants because they will be an echo of the voice of God to you. The only way you can know God's servants is to know the voice of God. If you don't know God's voice for yourself, you won't be able to discern the voice of God's servants and you will be in confusion. Christianity is not based on a mediatorship of priesthood, other than the priesthood of the Lord Jesus Christ. You need to know Him for yourself, and then you will receive of the ministries He supplies for you in the Body.

Proverbs 24:3 talks about building, as we build and grow in the Body of Christ and in our relationship with the Lord. "Through wisdom is a house builded; and by understanding it is established." Therefore, we need to seek wisdom and understanding in our walk with God. The church is in a restoration period in which all of these feasts are being re-established, and THOSE GOVERNING THE SECOND COMING OF CHRIST ARE NOW BEGINNING TO BE KEPT FOR THE FIRST TIME IN THE HISTORY OF THE CHURCH. We need to look at some truths in the Scriptures which come from the prophets and men of restoration concerning the restoration of Israel after they were in Babylonian captivity. The church is definitely coming out of Babylon, which means religious confusion. There are countless churches in Marin County which by their label would be called Christian but which teach about yoga, astrology, spiritism and all kinds of things that are antichrist because they don't know truth. However, this restoration period has been one in which the church has been coming out of Babylon into truth. The books of Ezra, Nehemiah, Haggai and Zechariah need to be studied in this hour because they hold very precious truths that relate to what God is doing today.

> And when the seventh month was come, and the children of Israel were in the cities, the people gathered themselves together as one man to Jerusalem [the Feast of Tabernacles]. Ezra 3:1

> And when the builders laid the foundation of the temple of the Lord, they set the priests in their apparel with trumpets, and the Levites the sons of Asaph with cymbals, to praise the Lord, after the ordinances of David king of Israel. And they sang together by course in praising and giving thanks unto the Lord; because he is good, for his mercy endureth forever toward Israel. And all the people shouted with a great shout, when they praised the Lord, because the foundation of the house of the Lord was laid. Ezra 3:10–11

This is one of many passages showing the kind of worship that was typical of the church moving into these areas.

> Then they came to Zerubbabel, and to the chief of the fathers, and said unto them, Let us build with you: for we seek your God, as ye do; and we do sacrifice unto him since the days of Esarhaddon king of Assur, which brought us up hither. But Zerubbabel, and Jeshua, and the rest of the chief of the fathers of Israel, said unto them, Ye have nothing to do with us to build an house unto our God; but we ourselves together will build unto the Lord God of Israel, as king Cyrus the king of Persia has commanded us. Ezra 4:2–3

> Be it known now unto the king that, if this city be builded, and the walls set up again, then will they not pay toll, tribute, and custom, and so thou shalt endamage the revenue of the kings. Ezra 4:13

Opposition came as they began to build the tabernacle. They were looking to the fulfillment of Tabernacles and began to build accordingly so that the temple would have everything in place, at the culmination of which the presence of God would come. Then someone raised their head and said, "If these Israelites do this, they're not going to pay tribute to the Babylonian kingdom."

"No, you can't worship that way, you can't have that spiritual liberty and privilege." That has been true all over the world, but it hasn't been true in America until this last decade when the government of the United States, through different agencies, has been challenging Christian privileges and constitutional rights. All across the country, churches have been brought into court for violating laws which try to say that Christian day schools are not religious activities, while the Constitution says that the government will not make any laws to regulate or support religion. We are facing this kind of opposition for the first time in the history of America. As the church comes out of its religious confusion and realizes that it has forsaken its responsibilities to the youth and children of its generation, we are finding opposition. The state says that the children don't belong to the parents but to the state. They are trying to tell us that we have to turn our children over to a godless system of education that teaches antichrist doctrine. In the late 1960's secular humanism was defined as a religion by the Supreme Court of the United States because it met every single regulation to define a religion in our country. This has become the state religion.

This is opposition from without. When we build the young people of this country so that they know the truth of Jesus Christ and have spiritual reality, this country will not be able to continue in the antichrist patterns as the enemy desires. However, if the minds of the youth are taken and corrupted so that there is an acceptance of alternate lifestyles and a destruction of the concept of nuclear families, and if the concept of any source of morality is ridiculed and destroyed, then the state becomes the god. *This is what they were fighting in Ezra's day, and this is what we are fighting today.*

And the Levites *caused the people to understand the law:* and the people stood in their place. So they read in the book in the law of God distinctly, *and gave the sense, and caused them to understand the reading.* Neh. 8:7–8

Then he said unto them, Go your way, eat the fat, and drink the sweet, and send portions unto them for whom nothing is prepared: for this day is holy unto our Lord: neither be ye sorry; for the joy of the Lord is your strength. Neh. 8:10

This all occurred at the time of the Feast of Tabernacles. They got into the Word of God, they prepared for those who didn't have, they began to give and they began to rejoice in the Lord.

And that they should publish and proclaim in all their cities, and in Jerusalem, saying, Go forth unto the mount, and fetch olive branches, and pine branches, and myrtle branches, and palm branches, and branches of thick trees, to make booths, as it is written. Neh. 8:15

Also day by day, from the first day unto the last day, he read in the book of the law of God. And they kept the feast seven days; and on the eighth day was a solemn assembly, according unto the manner.
Neh. 8:18

THEY WERE LEARNING TO BATTLE BY KEEPING THE FEAST. They read and kept the law, and as they did the Scripture says they battled and that the battle was from within and from without.

We're talking about warfare. As long as you stay back with what God did 50 or 100 years ago, you won't have any war. As long as you don't rock the boat and challenge the powers of darkness and speak the truth fully as it is, you won't have war. The enemy comes as soon as you do something. A beautiful picture of this is of Paul after he was shipwrecked. On the island they took some wet boards to start a fire and a viper came out and latched onto Paul's arm. As soon as you get the fire of the Holy Spirit to move somewhere, every viper in hell will stick his head out! WE CANNOT BE AFRAID OF THE RESISTANCE OF THE ENEMY BECAUSE FEAR HAS KEPT SO MUCH OF THE CHURCH IN A PLACE OF INEFFECTIVENESS.

Who is left among you that saw this house in her first glory? and how do you see it now? Is it not in your eyes in comparison of it as nothing? Yet now be strong, O Zerubbabel, saith the Lord; and be strong, O Joshua, son of Josedech, the high priest; and be strong, all ye people of the land, saith the Lord, and work: for I am with you, saith the Lord of hosts:

173

According to the word that I covenanted with you when ye came out of Egypt, so my spirit remains among you: fear ye not. For thus saith the Lord of hosts; Yet once, it is a little while, and I will shake the heavens, and the earth, and the sea, and the dry land; And I will shake all nations, and the desire of all nations shall come: and I will fill this house with glory, saith the Lord of hosts. The silver is mine, and the gold is mine, saith the Lord of hosts. The glory of this latter house shall be greater than of the former, saith the Lord of hosts: and in this place will I give peace, saith the Lord of hosts. Hagg. 2:3-9

Many people now look at the church and say, "Where's all the glory and the power that the early church had?" However, the prophecy said that God would once more shake the heavens and the earth, THE SEEMINGLY EMPTY TEMPLE WOULD BECOME FILLED WITH THE GLORY OF GOD AND THE GLORY OF THE LATTER HOUSE WOULD BE GREATER THAN THAT OF THE FORMER. He prophesied and comforted saying, "My Spirit is with you, fear not, BE STRONG."

Finally, my brethren, be strong in the Lord, and in the power of his might. Eph. 6:10

In II Timothy the same thing is said concerning warfare: "Now therefore, my son, be strong in the grace that is in Christ Jesus" — an exhortation to be strong in the face of opposition and spiritual battle. **THE SONS OF GOD ARE GOING TO MOUNT UP WITH WINGS AS EAGLES IN THIS LAST HOUR AND WILL TAKE UNTO THEMSELVES THEIR GOD-GIVEN AUTHORITY IN THE SPIRIT WORLD. MEN AND WOMEN OF GOD WHO KNOW HOW TO WAR IN THE SPIRIT, WHO KNOW WHO THEY ARE, WHO DON'T RUN EVERY TIME THE ENEMY STICKS UP HIS HEAD AND ROARS, WILL BATTLE AND WRESTLE WITH SPIRITUAL WEAPONS UNTIL THEY TAKE THE VICTORY.**

Right now the political arena is shaking, the financial arena is shaking, the physical, natural realm is shaking; in every area God is beginning to shake the heavens and the earth so that which is unshakeable might remain. The prophecy of Zecchariah speaks of how it's not by might nor by power, but by God's Spirit. It will not be by your denominational background, as much as you may have appreciated it in the past and what it has meant to you in your life. It is not going to be by someone's religious method, nor is it going to be by home studies or cell groups, FOR IT'S NOT BY MIGHT NOR BY POWER, BUT BY MY SPIRIT, SAITH THE LORD! He may use some of these things, but let's get our eyes where they belong. Let us begin to realize that we are in a spiritual warfare, and denominational nametags and man-made methods mean nothing. Either God is with you and intervening in your life or He is not.

As we go on to keep Atonement and from there to Tabernacles and find the fullness of the glory of God coming into the temple, we will have to understand what it means to battle and to stand steady in the battle. *We have to understand how to stand without fear.* How did they overcome the enemy, according to Revelation 12? They overcame him by the blood of the Lamb, by the word of their testimony and they loved not their lives unto the death. Those who are going to go on and keep this feast and see the glory of God will have to understand the connection with warfare. TRUMPETS WAS A CALL TO WAR; TABERNACLES IS A GREAT VICTORY OF SPIRITUAL WAR, FOR AT ITS CULMINATION IS THE MILLENNIAL REIGN WHEN CHRIST RETURNS PHYSICALLY WITH HIS SAINTS TO OVERTHROW THE ANTICHRIST KINGDOM. The word "glory" is a warrior's term. You see it in competitive games. Look at any major sporting event and the winners are in their glory. They have just demonstrated their expertise and superiority in whatever they did; they were the *best* at whatever it was. The concept of the King of Kings and Lord of Lords in Jesus Christ is related to the fact that He is sovereign over the heavens and the earth, and every rebellious voice of the enemy will be put down and the glory of God will be revealed.

> If you be reproached for the name of Christ, happy are ye; for the spirit of glory and of God rests upon you: on their part he is evil spoken of, but on your part he is glorified. I Peter 4:14

Once again, the word "glory" is tied right in to the concept of warfare. Remember, **Jesus came the first time as the Lamb for sinners slain, but He's coming back as the mighty Lion of the Tribe of Judah. He's coming back not as the Redeemer but as the King to take the purchased possession. He's coming to occupy!**

There is much effort involved between where we are and the point which we see in God's Word. To go from here through the Day of Atonement is an awesome thing. It's very uncomfortable to look at ourselves as we really are; however, if we want vitality and a reality of relationship with God that is alive, communicative and conscious, it requires a willingness to allow the Spirit of God to deal with us no matter how uncomfortable it is. We must be willing to endure the changing process. Despise the shame, but look forward unto Jesus, the author and finisher of our faith.

Father, we thank you for your word. We've gone through this series to see that the things at this end of the prophetic stream are as valid as those at the beginning that have already been fulfilled so minutely. Lord, we know that as we worship you in the pattern of truth exposed in the Word, as we move in hunger to see your glory and fullness come into the temple and face the opposition that is most definitely before us in the spirit, our hearts are mindful of the words of the prophet: to be strong, to fear not, that it's not by might nor by power but it's by your Spirit. Teach us, Lord, how to walk and how to war and how to abide in your Spirit.

JESUS AT THE FEAST
OF TABERNACLES

Let us now look at Jesus as He visited Jerusalem during the Feast of Tabernacles. Every movement of Jesus Christ was significant and important. He was God manifested in human flesh. Everywhere Jesus went, every attitude, behavior and action or inaction was an expression of the will and desire of the Father. Everything that was written, therefore, is of utmost importance. Every record of the Lord in the Scripture is vital because it met with the abridging process by which the things of His life were reduced for this written record as the Word of God. It is written multidimensionally in meaning in order to bring understanding to us by the Spirit.

Remember, we have a sequence of events. At Passover we saw that Israel came out of Egypt and kept Unleavened Bread and Firstfruits and entered into the law covenant at Mount Sinai on the Day of Pentecost. As they journeyed in the land and the tabernacle was set up, they kept the Feast of Tabernacles with its feasts of Trumpets, Day of Atonement and Booths.

We have seen that there was a prophetic aspect fulfilled in Christ. He was crucified on Passover, buried on Unleavened Bread, rose again on Firstfruits and the outpouring of the Holy Spirit took place on the Day of Pentecost. You and I as Christians should have kept Passover and gone on to keep Unleavened Bread and Firstfruits, dealing with our co-crucifixion with Christ, and Pentecost with the Baptism of the Holy Spirit.

WE FIND FOR THE FIRST TIME IN HISTORY THAT THE EVENTS SPOKEN OF BY THE LAST THREE FEASTS ARE NOW BEGINNING TO TAKE PLACE. THESE FEASTS GOVERN THE EVENTS SURROUNDING THE SECOND COMING OF CHRIST. FOR ISRAEL, THE FEAST OF TRUMPETS WOULD MEAN THE REGATHERING OF THE NATION, WHICH WE HAVE SEEN IN OUR DAY. THIS FEAST ALSO CARRIED WITH IT THE CHARISMATIC RENEWAL IN THIS CENTURY. IT IS A CALL TO KEEP THE OTHER FEASTS, A CALL TO SPIRITUAL WARFARE, A CALL TO GO ON WITH GOD TO COMPLETION, AND A CALL TO COME OUT OF OUR DENOMINATIONAL BACKGROUNDS AND IDENTIFY IN THE UNITY OF THE

BODY OF CHRIST. We see that this is the season the church has been experiencing during the decade of the '70's.

The next feast to be kept is Day of Atonement. We have learned that this feast is SIGNIFICANT OF RIGHTEOUSNESS BEING IMPLEMENTED IN OUR LIVES, and that is why the emphases in the Word and by the Spirit of this hour concern **relationships, integrity, holiness and the fruits of the Spirit.** Those things are being dealt with in each of our lives in a very beautiful way and at an awesome rate in order to change and prepare us to keep the Day of Atonement. When that hour of maturation comes, we will enter into a place of sanctification and victory over the flesh and over sin such as the church has never known.

We have seen that the consequence of keeping the Day of Atonement was the Feast of Booths. We have looked at it in terms of the glory of God coming to the temple and the restoration of the truths that we have studied. This commentary now deals with what is learned from the life of Jesus when He attended the Feast of Tabernacles, for His life tells us something of its meaning.

> Now the Jews' feast of tabernacles was at hand. His brethren therefore said unto him, Depart hence, and go into Judea, that thy disciples also may see the works that you do. John 7:2–3

> But when his brethren were gone up, *then went he also* up unto the feast, not openly, but as it were *in secret.* John 7:10

Under the heading of Feast of Tabernacles, the Feast of the Day of Trumpets took place on the first day of the month. The Feast of the Day of Atonement was on the tenth day of the month, Tabernacles beginning the very next day and continuing for seven days, followed by a second sabbath, making it eight days. It was the week after Atonement that the above passage is speaking of. Jesus didn't announce His coming, and the fact that He came secretly is very significant. The Scripture teaches us that the Lord's coming is a spiritual visitation in the midst of His people, as well as a literal and bodily visitation. CHRIST IS COMING **IN** HIS PEOPLE IN HIS FULLNESS BEFORE HE IS COMING **FOR** HIS PEOPLE PHYSICALLY. Those who are not born of the Spirit are blinded to the Kingdom of God, which is why He said in John 14,

178

"Where I go you shall see me, but the world, they will see me no more." **His coming secretly is significant of His spiritual visitation.**

> Be patient therefore, brethren, unto the coming of the Lord. Behold, the husbandman waits for the precious fruit of the earth, and has long patience for it, until he receives the early and latter rain. Be ye also patient; stablish your hearts: for the coming of the Lord draws nigh. James 5:7–8

The husbandman, who is the Father, is waiting for an outpouring of the Spirit that will bring the fruit to maturation, and at that time you will see the coming of the Lord. What James is saying speaks of a maturation. We should have both kinds of fruit, the fruit of souls won to Christ and the fruit of the Spirit, or Christian character. The building of this fruit comes through the moving of the Spirit. James is saying that this time of Tabernacles speaks of a MARVELOUS MOVE OF THE SPIRIT THAT WILL BRING INTO MATURATION THE FRUIT OF THE SPIRIT, A DIMENSION OF THE CHARACTER OF GOD, THE LIKENESS AND IMAGE OF CHRIST IN THE BELIEVER THAT HAS NOT PREVIOUSLY EXISTED AND, AS A RESULT, RELEASE AN EFFECTIVENESS IN TOUCHING A LOST AND DYING WORLD AND SEEING PEOPLE REAPED INTO THE KINGDOM OF GOD.

> For we have not followed cunningly devised fables, when we made known to you the power and coming of our Lord Jesus Christ, but were eyewitnesses of his majesty. For he received from God the Father honor and glory, when there came such a voice to him from the excellent glory, This is my beloved Son, in whom I am well pleased. And this voice which came from heaven we heard, when we were with him in the holy mount. I Peter 1:16–17

Peter is talking here about the experiences recorded in Matthew 17 on the Mount of Transfiguration, where Jesus had taken Peter, James and John. As He talked with Elijah and Moses, His clothes shone with the brightness of the sun because of the power and glory manifest at the transfiguration. Peter immediately recognized it as symbolic of the meaning of Tabernacles, for he said, "Let us build three booths here." Peter takes the manifestation of Christ in the transfiguration and relates it to Tabernacles and to the power and the coming of the Lord Jesus Christ. The apostle says that the coming of the Lord Jesus Christ is going to be likened unto what happened to Him on the Mount of Transfiguration, where the power and the glory of God were manifested so much in the physical realm that even the clothes that Jesus wore were shining with the brightness of the sun!

The three apostles who we are looking at here are the three who were with Jesus on the Mount. James talked about it in terms of the fruit that would come; Peter talked about it as the glory that was seen on the Mount; and John speaks of it in I John 3:

> Behold, what manner of love the Father hath bestowed upon us, that we should be called the sons of God: therefore the world knows us not, because it knew him not. Beloved, now are we the sons of God, and it does not yet appear what we shall be: but we know that, when he shall appear, we shall be like him; for *we shall see him as he is.* And every man that has this hope in him purifies himself, even as he is pure.
> I John 3:1–3

John recognizes that this is keeping the Day of Atonement, righteousness implemented. Peter associated the power and coming of Christ with the glory of God that appeared at Christ's transfiguration. James and John also spoke of the time of the Feast of Tabernacles and the manifestation of Christ within His people. James talks about faith without works being dead — let's get the fruit, the character, the glory! It is no wonder, for it is they who saw this glory of Christ on the Mount. We find that being made like Him in the hour of His spiritual visitation is in the hearts of His people. **Tabernacles is the visitation of Christ coming in His fullness within His people. It is the appearing of Christ within His temple and their consequent transformation after His likeness by beholding Him as He is.**

> But we all, with open face beholding as in a glass the glory of the Lord, are changed into the same image from glory to glory, even as by the Spirit of the Lord.
> II Cor. 3:18

We will see the glory of God after the Spirit at the coming of Christ in this spiritual visitation. It will have a consequence of transfiguring the believer, and in that metamorphosis we will be found in His likeness and image because we will see Him as He is. *Notice that this transfiguration is not by rapture but by the Spirit.* I'm challenging an old standard concept of Christianity. For years Christians have thought, well, you get saved, maybe water baptized, maybe even filled with the Holy Spirit and you don't smoke or chew or run with those who do, you sit in the pew and be a good person and then when Jesus comes, you'll be found in His likeness at the rapture and get all that God has for you. This is what has been taught in many churches, but nowhere does the Scripture teach us that we are transformed into Christian character by the rapture. It occurs by the Spirit through the Word of God and through the ministries that God has for us. Rapture is the consequence of that transformation, for we are transfigured into that same image, from glory to glory, even as by the Spirit of the Lord.

> Arise, shine; for thy light is come, and the glory of the Lord is risen upon thee. For, behold, the darkness shall cover the earth, and gross darkness the people: but the Lord shall arise upon thee, and his glory shall be seen upon thee. And the Gentiles shall come to thy light, and kings to the brightness of thy rising.
> Isa. 60:1-3

Isn't this what James said? THROUGH THE OUTPOURING OF HIS SPIRIT WILL COME THE FRUIT OF THE SPIRIT — CHRISTIAN CHARACTER, THE GLORY OF GOD SEEN IN US — AND, AS A RESULT, A GREAT HARVEST OF SOULS.

> Say to them that are of a fearful heart, Be strong, fear not: behold, your God will come with vengeance, even God with a recompense; he will come and save you. Then the eyes of the blind shall be opened, and the ears of the deaf shall be unstopped. Then shall the lame man leap as a hart, and the tongue of the dumb sing: for in the wilderness shall waters break out, and streams in the desert. Isa. 35:4-6

In the context of what Tabernacles had come to mean to Peter, James and John, it is very significant that Christ should be making His visit in this last great feast in secret. The significance is tied to the fact that the first approach at the coming of Christ is after the Spirit before it is after the flesh.

181

On the night that Jesus was betrayed, He shared some of the most intimate conversation He ever shared with His disciples. I have repeatedly studied the Scriptures concerning that night and His conversation with the disciples because they are packed full of truth and meaning.

> Let not your heart be troubled: ye believe in God, believe also in me. In my Father's house are many mansions: if it were not so, I would have told you. I go to prepare a place for you. John 14:1–2

The mansions here do not speak of some nice home in Marin County or of a beautiful home in the sky with nice pillars, fountains, swimming pools and hot tubs. In fact, the word "mansions" is a translator's error. The same Greek word that is translated "mansions" here is translated "place" later in the verse and "abode" later in this chapter, and it really means "abiding place." Christ is saying that there are many placements in His Father's family, placements of spiritual union with the Father and with the Son. As Jesus was preparing His disciples for this on that last night, He prayed:

> That they all may be one; as thou, Father, art in me, and I in thee, that they also may be one in us: that the world may believe that you have sent me. And the glory which thou gavest me I have given them; that they may be one, even as we are one: I in them, and thou in me, that they may be made perfect in one; and that the world may know that thou hast sent me, and hast loved them, as thou hast loved me.
> John 17:21–23

The placement that He is talking about here is one of relationship with Himself and with the Father that is a union of life. It is a placement of relationship that Christ in His incarnation demonstrated between Himself and His Father, a union that was so intimate that He said, "The words that I speak to you I speak not of myself but I received a commandment of the Father what I should say and what I should speak. The works that I do, it is not I that do them, it is the Father that dwells in me. I do nothing of myself but what I see my Father do, that is what I do." **Now He is saying, "I want you to come into a placement in the family where you have this relationship. I am going to prepare a way for you to have the same union of life with me and with the Father that I have exhibited before you."**

If ye had known me, ye should have known my Father also: and from henceforth ye know him, and have seen him. Philip said unto him, Lord, show us the Father, and it suffices us. Jesus said unto him, Have I been so long time with you, and yet hast thou not known me, Philip? he that hath seen me hath seen the Father; and how sayest thou then, Show us the Father?
John 14:7-9

Jesus was saying, If you've really seen what I am, if you've really seen me inside this physical house, if you've seen my heart, my motivation, my desires, my attitudes, then you have seen the Father also, because I and the Father are one.

Believest thou not that I am in the Father, and the Father in me? The words that I speak unto you I speak not of myself: but the Father that dwells in me, he does the works. Believe me that I am in the Father, and the Father in me: or else believe me for the very works' sake. Verily, verily, I say unto you, He that believes on me, the works that I do shall he do also; and greater works than these shall he do; because I go unto my Father. John 14:10-12

I will not leave you comfortless: I will come to you. Yet a little while, and the world sees me no more; but you see me: because I live, you shall live also. At that day you shall know that I am in my Father, and you in me, and I in you. John 14:18-20

The key to this secret visitation, or vital union, is given in verses 21-23. Look at verse 23:

Jesus answered and said unto him, If a man love me, he will keep my words: and my Father will love him, and we will come unto him, and make our abode with him.

"We will take up residence within him; there will be a degree of union of life, of oneness. I am coming after the Spirit and the world won't recognize me because the world is dead and blind spiritually, but you will live because I live and therefore you will see me. If you will hear my words and keep them as I speak to your life, then I will love you; and if you love me then you will keep my words. If you will keep my words, I will love you and my Father will love you, and out of that love commitment, because of the expression of keeping my word, we will come to you and will take up residence within you with our manifest presence!"

I am trying to show you that biblically, the concept of Christ coming secretly, or in a way in which the world does not recognize Him, *is significant of the fact that He is coming by spiritual visitation.* Those who have eyes to see will see, those who have ears to hear will hear what the Spirit says unto the church.

There are many abodes in the Kingdom of Heaven, many placements in the Father's family. Much of it will depend upon the level of one's Christian maturity and character appropriated by faith and obedience. Not everyone is going to have the same placement in heaven. There are many placements in your own family; some of your family members are closer to you than others, and so it is in the Father's family.

> And when he was demanded of the Pharisees, when the kingdom of God should come, he answered them and said, The kingdom of God comes not with observation [outward appearance]. Luke 17:20

> Again, the kingdom of heaven is like unto treasure hid in a field [hidden from view], the which when a man has found, he hides, and for joy thereof does and sells all that he has, and buys that field. Matt. 13:44

In Christ's day, the Jews were looking for the Messiah to come and deliver them from the oppressive political rule of Rome, but that is not why Jesus came. He was there to bring a spiritual kingdom; the physical kingdom would follow at the Millennium. I see a great parallel. Today the Church of Jesus Christ in many corners is looking for a rapture to deliver them from earth's bondage and to establish them in a throne of power and authority! The Lord will come again in like manner as He was taken into heaven, but it's not all that you may think it is meant to be and not everyone who thinks he is going will go. There is something much more important to take place prior to the rapture. First there must be the appearing of Christ in His fullness within His people to establish the Kingdom of God in their hearts and in their lives. *That* is the hope of the church. Colossians 1 tells us, "This is the hope that has been withheld from the ages: Christ in you, the hope of glory." THE FULLNESS OF CHRIST IN YOU: THAT'S THE HOPE OF GLORY, not a change of a physical tabernacle, not a rapture into a new location. The hope of glory is the fullness of Christ formed in your spirit, and it doesn't come by observation, it comes by the Spirit.

Christ first visited the Feast of Tabernacles in secret before He revealed Himself openly. The Israelites were all rejoicing in this feast and were going through the daily sacrifices when Jesus showed up at the temple and began to teach but did not reveal His identity. He was like all of the other scribes who had come from different quarters throughout Israel to keep the feast. Christ stood in the court area where the scribes taught, opened the Word of God and taught them the truth of the Word, never declaring who He was. *They would have to know Him after the Spirit.*

Those who are in tune and who are walking with the Lord after the Spirit will find the Scripture is true that says the steps of a righteous man are ordered of the Lord. If you're walking after the Spirit and not playing church, if you're in right relationship with God and not compromising over certain issues, you will be in the right place at the right time and *you won't miss the hour of visitation.* However, there are many who name the name of Jesus throughout our churches in this land and around the world who will miss the hour of visitation because their lives aren't right with God and they're living in compromise. Hear this before it's too late.

> The Pharisees heard that the people murmured such things concerning him: and the Pharisees and the chief priests sent officers to take him. Then said Jesus unto them, Yet a little while am I with you, and then I go unto him that sent me. You shall seek me, and shall not find me: and where I am, thither you cannot come. Then said the Jews among themselves, Where will he go, that we shall not find him? Will he go unto the dispersed among the Gentiles, and teach the Gentiles? What manner of saying is this that he said, You shall seek me, and shall not find me: and where I am, you cannot come? John 7:32–36

They could not take Christ because it wasn't time — Christ would lay down His life, His life was not taken from Him. So also, I prophesy in the name of Jesus Christ that THE CHURCH WILL HAVE AN OPEN DOOR TO EVERY NATION IN

THE WORLD IN THIS LAST HOUR BEFORE THE PHYSICAL RETURN OF THE LORD, AND NOTHING SHALL BE IMPOSSIBLE TO HIM WHO BELIEVES. THERE WILL BE MAGISTRATES AND THOSE WHO WILL SEEK TO TAKE AND DELIVER GOD'S SERVANTS UNTO DEATH AND PRISON, BUT THEY WILL NOT BE ABLE TO DO SO UNTIL THE HOUR OF HARVEST IS FINISHED. GOD WILL OPEN DOORS BEHIND THE IRON CURTAIN, BEHIND THE BAMBOO CURTAIN IN THAT GREAT NATION OF CHINA, AND IN TIBET AND NEPAL WHERE YOU CANNOT GO IN AND FREELY PREACH THE GOSPEL TODAY. THESE DOORS WILL BE OPENED BY THE SPIRIT OF GOD FOR THOSE WHO WILL WALK AFTER THE SPIRIT AND THEY WILL MINISTER IN POWER, THEY WILL MINISTER IN GLORY, THEY WILL MINISTER IN AUTHORITY! THE AUTHORITIES WILL SEEK TO TAKE THEM BUT THEY WILL NOT BE ABLE TO TOUCH THEM IN THAT HOUR, FOR GOD WILL YET CAUSE THIS GOSPEL TO BE PREACHED IN THE DEMONSTRATION AND POWER OF THE SPIRIT AS A WITNESS TO **ALL** NATIONS BEFORE THE COMING OF THE LORD.

It is interesting to see what happened on the last day of the Feast of Tabernacles in Jesus' day. Dawn would come and the trumpets would be blown announcing the beginning of the day. It was a time of joy and hilarity, of feasting and joy and rejoicing that they could not have at other times in the year since they couldn't preserve or grow food in green houses like we do today. Each day at the morning sacrifice, they would offer an animal unto the Lord, the people would take palm branches and march around the altar of burnt offering as Israel did at Jericho. They would make an offering of commitment and consecration unto God and would march around it with their palm branches, a symbol of victory, once every morning. On the seventh day they marched around it seven times, as at Jericho. Then came the ceremony of the "pouring out of water." The priest took a vessel to the Pool of Salome at the time the sacrifice was to take place. He filled it with water and brought it back by way of the Pool of Bethesda in the midst of the joy and the blowing of trumpets. They would take that vessel of water and mix it with wine, a type of blood, and would pour it out by the altar and would read this prophecy from Isaiah:

Behold, God is my salvation; I will trust, and not be afraid: for the LORD JEHOVAH is my strength and my song; he also is become my salvation. Therefore with joy shall ye draw water out of the wells of salvation. Isa. 12:2–3

In the last day, that great day of the feast, Jesus stood and cried, saying, If any man thirst, let him come unto me, and drink. He that believeth on me, as the scripture hath said, out of his belly shall flow rivers of living water. (But this spake he of the Spirit, which they that believe on him should receive: for the Holy Ghost was not yet given; because that Jesus was not yet glorified). John 7:37–39

Right at the moment that the priest was carrying out the ceremony of the "pouring out of water," Jesus made this cry, "If any man thirst let him come unto me...." He was speaking prophetically about the RELEASE OF THE SPIRIT AT THE END OF THE FEAST OF TABERNACLES. IT WILL BE A GREAT RIVER OF LIFE BRINGING SALVATION, HEALING AND DELIVERANCE TO THE NATIONS OF THE WORLD.

Then said he unto me, These waters issue out toward the east country, and go down into the desert, and go into the sea: which being brought forth into the sea, the waters shall be healed. And it shall come to pass, that every thing that liveth, which moveth, whithersoever the rivers shall come, shall live: and there shall be a very great multitude of fish, because these waters shall come thither: for they shall be healed; and every thing shall live whither the river cometh. Ezek. 47:8–9

This river of the Spirit that Jesus is speaking of is the healing stream of Ezekiel. This is the hour that is about to break upon the church. It will be the greatest manifestation of the power and glory of God that the world has ever known and it will come at the end of the Feast of Tabernacles. At the climax of that great harvest will come the rapture!

Everywhere that Jesus went and poured out of His Spirit, something followed. Those who accepted received pardon and grace and deliverance, but those who rejected received judgment. He did most of His miracles in Bethesda and Chorazin and said at the end of His ministry, "Woe unto thee,

Bethesda and Chorazin. If the works that I had done in you had been done in Sodom and Gomorrah, they would have repented long ago in sackcloth and ashes." Throughout the Scripture, before every judgment period of God in the earth there is a period of tremendous grace and opportunity to repent. God does not want to judge, He wants to pardon. Those who see the grace and power and glory of God in its manifestation and reject it are left no other choice but the judgment of God. After the rapture of the church, the wrath of God during the tribulation period will be poured out on the earth against the antichrist and his kingdom as Jesus comes physically with His saints to set up His millennial kingdom on the earth.

We have seen the prophetic pattern from Passover to Unleavened Bread and Firstfruits, Pentecost, Trumpets — all fulfilled, Trumpets fulfilled in our day heading towards the Day of Atonement. The last three feasts of Trumpets, Day of Atonement and Booths are fulfilled in one generation, as were the first four. We are living in the generation that will not pass from planet earth until these things be fulfilled.

There is an exuberance, an exhilaration and an excitement that fills my spirit for the things in the Kingdom of God that we are privileged to participate in and to see in this generation. God is doing a new thing. Greater works are beginning to take place. There is a revival of Christianity taking place around the world. It's beginning; it's the river that Ezekiel spoke of. For those of us who are making a full effort to walk after God's will and to allow the Spirit of God to deal with us and change us, it's a time of great excitement and fulfillment. Those of you who have compromise in your commitment with God, a little bit of anxiety and fear grips your heart when we speak of these things, but it need not be that way. You can let the Holy Spirit deal with you and you can begin to have a turnaround in your heart and life. As the Apostle John said about this hour, everyone who has this hope in him purifies himself even as Christ is pure, and we need to allow the Spirit of God to work to remove every compromise. We should be in the place where we are letting the Spirit of God actively deal with us, where we are receptive. If you are resisting the work of God's Spirit in your life and you need to make a surrender to the Lord so that you will be ready for what God has prepared for you and not miss this hour of visitation, give Him your life afresh!

We know, Lord, that none of us has attained this fullness, but we are headed in that direction. Father, these who need to make a surrender to you want to be sure they are walking in a place of commitment to you without compromise, trusting you to make them ready for that hour, whereas the Scripture says, I know him whom I have believed and am persuaded that He is able to keep that which I have committed unto Him against that day. I am persuaded that in that hour I will be ready. As the Scripture says, He is able to present you faultless before His throne in glory. Lord, we commit ourselves to you against that day. Father, without reservation, we ask that you work in our hearts and our lives to prepare us, for Jesus' sake, Amen.